PSYCHIC NAZI HUNTER

A True Tale of an Incredible Life

The Story of Alan Wood-Thomas: Decorated War Hero, Acclaimed and Respected Artist, Loving Family Man, but he had a secret second life, one where he psychically tracked down Nazis and their collaborators.

HOLOCAUST: Simple minimalist drawing that shows the helplessness, yet strength, of the victim. Being lifted to the heavens while still tied to the earth, the artist offers a back breaking pose in one, pure line. Never Again.

Psychic Nazi Hunter
COPYRIGHT 2017   Michael Wallace
This book is published under the Berne Convention. All copyright protected to the author. No prior use without permission except for excerpts for review or educational purposes. All enquiries via Email to:
  info.numberharmonics@gmail.com
  Published by Ladder to the Moon Publications.
  ISBN 978-0-9941798-5-2
  All rights reserved to the copyright holder.

PSYCHIC NAZI HUNTER

Death to the Nazi!

ALAN WOOD-THOMAS: Psychic Nazi Hunter

How could an accepted and celebrated artist, a man who was a personal friend to Kerouac, Ginsberg and Harrison, somehow become embroiled in a world of espionage where he is hunting down Nazis? In this extraordinary book, Allan Wood-Thomas, decorated war hero, member of the French Resistance, artist, loving husband, and father to three children, reaches through the veil of secrecy to reveal his hidden self, the *Psychic Nazi Hunter!*

A more unlikely candidate you would never find. Taught as a youth by Jean Paul Sartre, recognised by Picasso, and yet embroiled in a world-wide hunt for the Nazis for twenty-five years: and no-one ever suspected!

Through the years many prominent people have purchased Alan Wood-Thomas works, including: Gregor Piatagorsky, famed cellist: Nicholas deB. Katzenbach, former Under Secretary of State and Attorney General of the US: Nelson Rockefeller: Ethel Kennedy, wife of Sen. Robert Kennedy: Christian Chapman, U.S. State department: and lifetime friend (Featured in "Secret Soldiers") Frederick Fox, former advisor to President Eisenhower.

During his years as an artist, Alan had many one man shows and had his art showcased at some renowned gallerys. As an Example: The Whitney Museum of American art in New York, The Art Institute of Chicago, the Tokyo Museum of Modern Art (which is now the National Museum of Modern Art), the Tel Aviv Museum of art in Tel Aviv, Israel and the Fransworth Museum in Rockland, Maine.

Alan was sold and exhibited through the Carlebach Gallery in New York when he was 28, as well as the John Heller Gallery, also in New York.

Other Books by this author:

Eat Your Fill / Eat Your Religion / Eat Your God Trilogy

The Book of Number Trilogy

Jermimiah Versus the Grabblesnatch

The Divinity Dice Series

Ratology: Way of the Un-Dammed

Ratology II: Who Gives a Rats?

Fragments of the Mirror

Water: More Precious than Gold

The Borringbar War

Hello Planet Earth

Available on Amazon or at
www.laddertothemoon.com.au

Contributors:

Cyrus Wood-Thomas: Articles and all background information regarding the story.

Alan Wood-Thomas: Cover Artwork and illustrations throughout the book. (Used with permission)

Linda LeBoutillier: Background references in her ongoing work with Cyrus Wood-Thomas, based on her book "Remote Assassin".

Many thanks also to Sarah Pascoe, step-grand-daughter of Alan Wood-Thomas, for her proof reading and oversight.

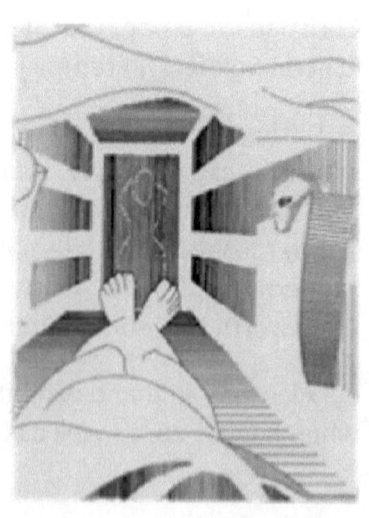

Index

Part One:

Red Leather Shoes 7
The Prodigal Son 14
Joining the Maquis 16
The Filing Cabinet 19
The Prodigal Son 21
Untold Secrets 24
Nazi Occupied Paris 27
Meeting Picasso 30
The Visions 33
Back to France 39
   December 1947 - Lyon 42
   Return to Paris 45
The Equipment 49
Assassination 54
New York - 1948 58
The Return to New York 61
The Philosophy of the Resistance 63
Camouflage 66
RESTITUTION 68
The Miami Job 71

Part Two:

The Final Nazi 75
The La Paz Assignment 79
At The Roemer House 83
The Accountant 86
The Gardener 89
Fascist Reunion 92
The Sums are Added, the Debt is Due 94
Panama Bound 98
The Final Solution 100
Connecticut 1976 103
The Kiss 105
Author Note: 107
Why Did So Many Nazis Go Unpunished? 109
MUNICH 112
POST SCRIPT 113
Dr Cyrus Wood-Thomas 113
Victims of Spoliations 116
About the Artist: 117

Note on Cover Portrait:

This portrait of Attorney General Katzenbach was the first Avant-Garde styled Portrait ever commissioned by the US Government. It marked a mile-stone in 1965 in what was considered as "acceptable" art by the establishment.

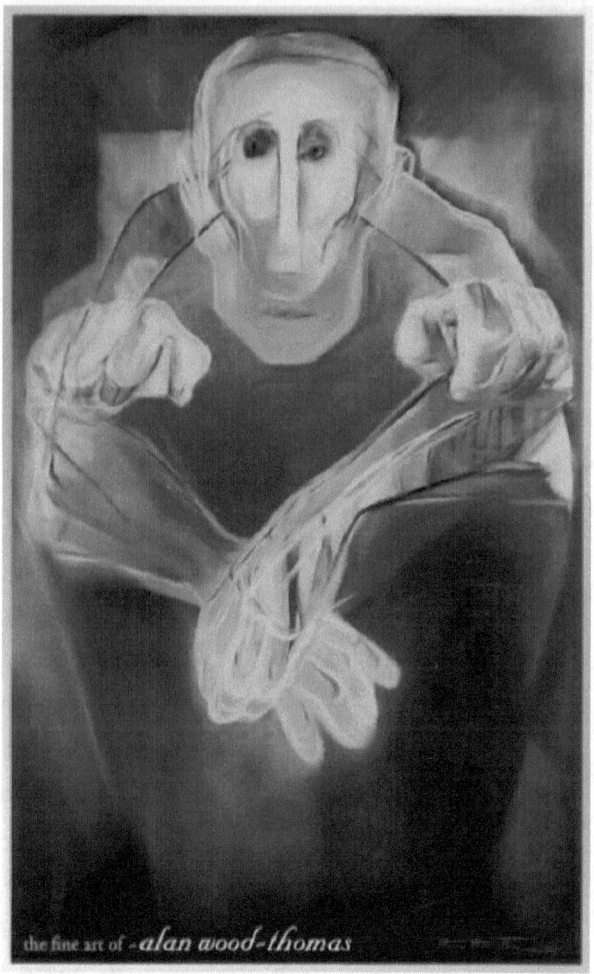

Alan Wood-Thomas often would talk about how he could see himself painting, from outside his body. This work above is titled "Astral Projection". It would seem he had an advanced ability to leave the body and discover things invisible to the ordinary man. Certainly it was what he used to track down the hidden Nazis in our society.

Red Leather Shoes

FBI Headquarters - Sometime in late 1965

J Edgar Hoover looked down admiringly at the fine red leather: such soft Italian workmanship wrapped around a hard shell Vamp made of salted leather. Bruno Magi, simple, well made and elegant. Some days he just wished he could wear them out of his office, but the ridicule. It was just a sad addiction, a dream. Instead, he confined the high heels to their usual resting place under his desk, taking comfort in the tight grip they had on his toes.

Before him, the troubling report. How could he have missed this for so long? A twenty-plus year project to eliminate former Nazis: World-wide, hundreds of Nazis in hiding had been assassinated in their beds, their throats cut. Clearly, a ritual execution.

Not that he minded, or cared about the Germans, but how could he have not known? He had made extensive inquiries, which led to a very curious end: Nicholas deB. Katzenbach, the current Attorney General. But apart from him being a former prisoner of war, with a natural inclination towards killing the Nazi, there was no hard information to connect him to the murders. Everything pointed there, but nothing stuck.

In all honesty, he did not even know why the man was happy to call by. The two men had no liking for each other, so why was he cooperating? Guilty men do not do this, and innocent men in his position are too busy. No solicitors, no-one else present, this was his only requirement. Of course, he knew it would be recorded. It didn't make sense.

Turning over a coin in his fingers, he asked for the man to be invited into his office. The door opens, and one of his enemies walk in. Tall, gaunt, square jawed, not a man to be trifled with, Katzenbach steps through and simply nods. No greeting. He sits where the secretary indicates, clearly not a man who was worried.

"Why am I talking to you, Mr. Katzenbach?" This style of disarming first question so often got people advertising their fears and worries in the first few sentences. But the man did not answer or even react. Hoover waited, nothing. "You are right, of course, rhetorical question, we know why you are here. Hundreds of German ex-military dead. Throats cut and executed without trial. I know you are connected, I don't know exactly how.

"Now I cannot threaten you, or imprison you, or do anything against you, Sir. To start with, I don't have the evidence, and all these crimes were committed outside of the US. Not my jurisdiction, but I would genuinely like to know HOW a highly efficient network of Nazi killers, one not connected to any known intelligence organization, has managed to stay hidden for so long?"

Katzenbach still said nothing, but gracefully accepted the black coffee brought in by yet another secretary. He simply sipped it and then took stock of the man before him while cleaning his glasses. Hoover was a dangerous fellow. He had a dirt list five miles long, full of photos and smears against almost every significant player in Washington. But the man had nothing to hang on himself.

He was a good upstanding member of the community, faithful to his wife, a loving father to his children. He was no gambler, had little need for money, nor any need for ostentatious displays of wealth. Neither did he have any interest in prostitutes or children, so the photographic evidence that Hoover had on so many of his colleagues only troubled the Attorney General when it came to prosecuting them.

Katzenbach was not rich, but well enough off. His father had also been Attorney General. A pedigree, with a record clear of any wrongdoing plus his income was from impeccable and verifiable sources, Katzenbach could stare blankly back at Hoover without any concern. Yet, looking at the FBI Director he came to the conclusion that, while he personally had nothing to fear, the man truly wanted to know more. Hoover was also saying, without saying it, that now he knew about this matter he could make life difficult.

Decades of living in the shadows could come to an end if this were handled wrong.

"I will verify that a group does exist. I can give you no names, no hard information. This is for the reason that I do not know who is involved. I have ONE contact, who keeps me up to date for reasons of his own, perhaps simply because I am a powerful man on Capitol Hill. I have nothing, really, other than the assurance that each elimination is thoroughly vetted and cross checked, and that there are no mistakes. The reason is simple: Many Nazi war criminals did not see a court, and as a consequence, these invisible assassins make sure their case is heard directly with the highest authority."

"Dammit Katzenbach!" J Edgar slammed a fist down on the desk. Still no response. That wasn't going to work, either. Changing tone, "Look, I know you are protective of your own, but there's just no way the State can sanction or condone the murder of men without some sort of evidence put to a trial. This cannot continue."

"And what exactly is not going to continue?" Katzenbach responded. "The fact you know nothing?"

Hoover knew who and what he was dealing with. This man was a major force. Hidden, buried in the layers of the bureaucracy were hundreds of his people. He had feelers in every department, even his own. "You know I can make things hard, you need to give me something. My job is to protect the American people, but this also means protecting the reputation and standing of the United States in the world. You are asking me to effectively turn a blind eye one of our citizens hunting down and killing Nazis. It is a thing that could blow up to become a major international incident. This I cannot allow. Will you help me here?"

The long line of the Katzenbach's nose showed a slight flare at the nostrils. Good, that got across. "Let's start with the HOW. How can some group without funding or intelligence find these bastards anyway? These Nazis are buried so deep in their little hidey-holes that they are not even on Santa's naughty list. NO ONE knew they were there, how did your people find them?"

"There are no 'my people' Mr. Hoover. There is no 'organization'. There are a few dedicated individuals, no more than twelve I am given to understand, and not all of them are even Jews. Please accept that I only know the rough outline of the business, but apparently, those involved are just ordinary men, living ordinary lives, who occasionally do something extraordinary." Katzenbach was fully aware he has essentially just breathed hot air up the arse of the FBI chief and had expected him to suck it up.

"This doesn't fly. There's no explanation of how it works: Where are they based? When is it planned? Who is involved? There is only the 'why it is done', which is obvious. Yes, we know they are Nazis, they deserve to die. But how are these ghosts of yours finding them when even 'I' with all the FBI at my disposal, cannot?"

"Well Mr. Hoover, you may just find it DOES fly, literally. I am about to tell you something you will, quite frankly, find almost impossible to believe. The man who finds these war criminals is not following any process you use. He is not a 'spy' in any current sense of the word, he uses no tracking of bank accounts, like the Jews. He does not involve himself talking to a target's family. Nothing he does follows any existing procedure. You have heard of 'remote viewing', yes? (Hoover nods, that Monroe absurdity again) This individual literally leaves their body, completely at random, and this is a process that is not even under their control. From what I am given to understand, he is taken by some force to where these men are hiding. And before you ridicule this, remember the facts. You cannot find these people, yet this one man I happen to know, can.

"I will add, he simply passes this information to a man who verifies it, a competent detective who lives outside the USA. It is his job in normal life to track down people who avoid the justice system, and so he has the tools to do so. Once the address of the war criminal is found by this unexplainable out-of-the-body method used by my confidant, a process is started. This is to verify the address, confirm who the individual was in their past life as a Nazi, or a collaborator, and to ascertain their level of guilt.

"Once it is clear that this man is a target, he is quietly dispatched by other unknown men whose job it was during World War Two to do just this. They see no difference between a dead Nazi then and a dead one now, and I am told that every single one of those who are, put down, (Katzenbach pauses, to emphasize the veterinary nature of the act) is responsible for the death of many Jews and other innocents." The Atourney General sits back in his chair, taking a proffered Gauloise. He smiles, it was his preferred tobacco. Hoover was telling him he had done his research. He lights up, and breaths in. Both men sit there, calmly assessing each other's reactions.

After the third red glow cools off on the cigarette, Hoover continues. "It may well be just as you say, but obviously I would frankly find all this a little too pat, and very difficult to believe. Without some sort of verifiable proof, I would have difficulty accepting any of this."

Here it is, the very reason Katzenbach agreed to this meeting. "Several weeks ago, well before you started making your inquiries, my contact happened to bump into me and out of the blue said you would ask to see me. He said had seen it, been there, flown above, and said that the proof you needed was very simple. Now, I have no idea what this next phrase means, but in order to help you believe, he told me I would need to tell you this: 'Red leather suits you'."

Hoover blinked. No one knew. It was his best kept and deepest secret. He refused to let his eyes go down, to look under the desk. Instead, he quietly kicks off his heels and slips his feet back into the austere black shoes every member of his administration wears. "And did he say what the outcome of this meeting would be?"

"Everything is a matter of choice, and what a person will choose in any given moment is not within his scope to predict, but he did say was that if the "Red Leather" comment made sense, then you would also understand that we all have certain aspects inherent in our nature that must remain hidden. Why? Because once revealed in open society they impede our ability to function."

The FBI chief sat there, absorbing what he had just been told. Was this a veiled threat? Changing tact once more, Hoover asked, "And how is this funded? More specifically: Are any government monies being tipped into this at any point along the line?"

"Exactly what I wondered about. There is no funding. Everyone involved does this of their own free will, and it is purely done as a volunteer. From what I am to understand, funds for travel and expenses are met by several committed parties, people completely removed from the process, but who advocate the final solution being applied to those who deserve it. Yes, they are mostly Jewish, but not tied to any external government or government agency. There are no significant cash outlays, there are no ties to government, and therefore no come back to yourself in any way."

"So you are saying I should just turn a blind eye?" Hoover snorted.

"With all due respect Mr. Hoover, you ARE blind. There's nothing for you to turn around to and find. And even if you could, what would you see? What you have are reports of Nazi war criminals dying, and it could be anyone, from anywhere, at any time. It could be the sister they raped as a child, taking revenge. It could be a wife, beaten, protecting her children from brutality. Anyone, from anywhere, acting at any time they choose. All you know is that they all die the same way, with their throats cut while they sleep. What I will tell you is this simple truth: that all of this hinges on the peculiar ability of one individual, and that it is something that even he does not fully understand.

"However, it DOES happen and continues to happen. Every month or so, this man is taken from his body and shown where one of these creatures live. He is an atheist, by the way, not even a Jew, and has no idea why he has been selected to do this. But as a former resistance fighter and a decorated US military officer, he has absolutely no qualms about passing the information he is given to individuals to verify it. He, of course, has full knowledge of what happens to the war criminal once his 'remote viewing' is proven accurate."

Hoover laughed at the absurdity of this. "Well, so you have yourself some sort of Psychic Nazi Hunter. Tell me, how often are his visions verified as being accurate?"

Katzenbach leans forward, stubs out the cigarette, and says, quietly. "100% accuracy. 100% verification, despite the target using name changes and plastic surgery. 100% efficiency."

This got Hoover's attention like nothing else. He had been laughing at Monroe and his insane claims, actively resisting the funding the military had been putting into his projects. But Katzenbach, though thoroughly unlikeable, was no fool. If this were true, if someone could spy with such accuracy without bugs, or the need to bribe people, what a doorway it opens for intelligence. "Can I meet with him?"

The answer is flat and final. "No."

"Why not?"

"Every single member of the organization is sworn to absolute secrecy. I only know because the man had a vision, and saw that you were talking to me. He approached me out of the blue only weeks ago. I had known the fellow for many years but had no idea about any of this. On a casual meeting, he simply broached it with me, saying that I would be brought to you here today.

"He merely gave me an outline of how it works, nothing else. The entire process is done in complete secrecy. No-one but the controller who verifies the sighting has any communication with the one who has the visions. I am told there are a number of men and apparently even women who perform a role in the execution, but that none of them know each other. And apparently, even the controller can be a different person on different tasks.

"It is a truly extraordinary thing, and there is no information about how any of this works that you could find because no-one other than the persons involved knows anything. Multiple people, all blind to each other, all unknowing of the source of the information, and they simply do their job."

Katzenbach made to get up out of the button-stitched brown leather chair, his arched eyebrow raised, asking without an actual question if there was anything further that Hoover needed.

There was. J Edgar laughs, "So why did he tell you, or me, anything? If this is so secret, why did the man risk letting you in?"

"I am not 'in'. Further, as a good citizen, I am simply passing along information as it was given to me to the man who would be most concerned about it. I have no idea why this individual told me. I gather he had his reasons, but these I am not privy to." The Attorney General of the United States, the man most committed to upholding the rule of Law looked back at the FBI Chief.

Hoover just nodded, but added, "You know if this gets out, if anyone is found committing these acts, then the entire show will be gone over with a fine tooth comb. I am not making any offers of impunity, nor making any deals."

"We will both be long gone before anyone even hears a whisper of this ghost. Trust me, you can go over every person I have met within the last few weeks, and you will think I must have lied. So you will go back a few months, then a year. You will still have absolutely no clue who it might be, and this information I have passed on will only ever remain as an innocuous chat two men had regarding an odd report you received." With this, the Attorney General stood up, shook Hoover's hand, and turned to walk away.

But as he turned to leave, Hoover spoke up, "And of course, everything you have said here in this room could well be all a red herring to distract me from the mess that all this civil rights crap of yours is creating."

Katzenbach looked back and smiled a crocodile smile. "Of course."

The man left, Hoover sat there thinking. Katzenbach knew too much about the story to have not been involved to some degree, in some way. Possibly he was the one who organized funding, that seemed most likely. Other than that, the man was right. All he really had to go one was an assessment by an operative who connected dots between the death of suspected Nazis over the last twenty years.

Resistance fighter? Maquis assassins always cut the throat of the Nazi or the collaborator, but there was no way to find out any of those. The French Resistance was officially long over, with no records, and the French Government was entirely uncooperative anyway.

Was he being thrown a distraction? The Civil Right Bill was up in months, and maybe this was being used as an irresistible fish to chase, something to get him looking at other stuff. Damn that fool Kennedy, opening this can of worms which consumed so much of his time. Then he gets himself shot, and Katzenbach forces the FBI into an open inquiry into the man's assassination. More time eating distractions.

He put the file away. Not enough information, no proof, no clear direction for an investigation. But beyond all these question marks, the fact that this "spy" knew about his shoes? This was something to follow up.

Over his shoulder, as Katzenbach left, he heard Hoover's voice speaking into his intercom, "Get Munroe on the line, Miss Crenshaw."

Man is nothing else but what he purposes, he exists only in so far as he realizes himself, he is therefore nothing else but the sum of his actions, nothing else but what his life is.
Jean-Paul Sartre

The Prodigal Son

At the End of Times, the Beginning

Cyrus had the letter in hand as he stepped from the taxi at 138 South Main Street, Westbrook, Connecticut. The extraordinary man who fathered him was dying. He had immediately taken leave of absence from the Sorbonne, and left Paris to be with him. He really did not know why, but an inner compulsion drove him. His father must not die alone.

Stepping up the wooden stairs of the last century house, they creaked under his foot, giving warning to all inside that someone approached. But no-one stirred. He looked back at the uncared for lawn, over the nature reserve to the Patouche River. It was a beautiful place to die. He went to the door and knocked, but there was no response. Mother must be out. Moving along the veranda, he looked in the room with the open french doors, and there was his father, asleep.

Silently he stepped in, and sat in a reading chair, watching the old man breath. And sitting there, he began to wonder. All those stories the man had told to him when growing up, all the secrecy he had been sworn to, were they real? And if they were, perhaps this is how it had been done? Just walk in the open door of a house in a sleepy provincial town, and cut the throat of the collaborator. All those extraordinary tales he had been told of his father's friends from the Marquis hunting down the Nazi and their collaborators after the war, were they ay least in part true?

The eyes opened, registering no surprise. Alan Wood-Thomas gazed into space. Lou Gehrig's Disease was stealing the last of his enormous vitality, and he knew he was not long for this world. His son, his only confidant, yet so young. He sat there, a good boy, all the way from Paris to be with his father. He felt proud, so very proud. "Is there anything you would like to know about my life?" He asked, not even saying "Hello" or "How was the trip" or "Thank you for coming".

Cyrus just sat there, not speaking. Well, perhaps he had told him enough. The old man waited. Finally, the lad spoke up, "All those Nazis. You said you were instrumental in their death. Yet you are a respected well-known artist. Exhibited at Carlbach's, known and loved by Ginsberg, Kerouac, and others. The leading lights of the artistic world welcomed you. I find it difficult to reconcile the two lives. Didn't you ever feel a conflict in what you did?"

The old man looked over. He was full of ideals in his youth. But this lot didn't see the horrors of the Nazis. It wasn't just the Jews. It wasn't only how they abused his beloved teacher, Jean-Paul Sartre. It wasn't simply the fact that he, as a member of the French Resistance, had a duty in this matter. It was the cold hard reality that the Nazis represented a curse that blackened society.

Before the war, at sixteen in the Spanish Civil war with the Marquis, he saw fascists at work, and right from the start he knew he had a duty to serve France and protect her from these madmen. And this meant ending the life of those who were her enemy. "Why would I have a conflict? These people are the scum of the earth, and allowing them to continue to breed, to live? Now this would be a crime, a crime against humanity."

He could see that it wasn't getting through. The boy needed to know more. "Cyrus my boy, you are still young. I was never young, at sixteen I killed my first man, not directly, but I was already in Spain, fighting for the resistance in the Civil War. My actions caused men to die and I had already seen first-hand what evil can lie in the heart of a fascist. And later, the War itself. I have seen the files the Nazis had, of the innocents they were sending to the death camps, guilty because they were gay, or Jewish or Slav. When you see pure evil, there is no conflict. There are no questions about what you must do.

"But even if there were doubts, which I did not have, surely the visions sent to me were in themselves a message to continue. I did not ASK for these, my boy. I did not ASK to be shown where the Nazis were hiding out. I did not ASK for the role I took on in secret. I was given this, and I accepted that it was my task in this life to not just paint pretty pictures, but to DO something that made this world better.

"Do I have a regret? Absolutely not. It was my true purpose in this life."

The child still did not get it. Alan looked inside, saw the limited time he had left, and decided to answer the question his son never asked, the story of his life. Someone had to know, he had to entrust his secrets to at least one Soul, and his boy returning from Paris was the sign he needed.

Taking a deep breath, knowing they were alone, he began. "You can blame Sartre. This is where it started, in Paris. It was 1937, a few years before the war. I was attending philosophy lectures at the Lycee where he was teaching. When the Spanish Civil War broke out, it was he who convinced this sixteen-year-old boy, and others like me, to DO something with his life. Mostly because of him, I went to Spain to join the Marquis."

Cyrus's father began his tale at the beginning.

Joining the Maquis

The Spanish Civil War

Alan Wood-Thomas gathered up his memories from where they had fallen along the path of his life. "Sartre was an advocate of responsibility, personal responsibility and an opponent of any autocratic regime that restricted the rights of the people. Myself and a small group of kids stayed to listen after his lectures, to get what he saw as the real education we needed. I remember his words ... "

"A man makes a knife. He has intention, focus, purpose. This evolves into the thing of function that he creates, the knife. And so in the making of the object, its purpose already exists. It is found within itself. But who made the man who made the knife? You are born not BY design, you are born INTO design. This is the social order around you. Do you subsume your society and become what is ITS intention? Or do you define yourself?

"The truest evil is the one that steals this choice from a man. I have been to Berlin, I have seen what the Nazi are doing. They are like the man who is making a knife, they are creating a society where people are beaten into a purpose. The burden of freedom is taken away, those who are different are castigated.

"The Civil War in Spain is now a place where some in that society are choosing to define themselves, to take the terrible choices. We ask if this is any of our business, but I say that now we are AWARE, it is a reality we must either affirm or deny. Our Government is weak, the leaders are weak, and the harsh reality is that the strong will consume the weak. We must defend Spain and her freedom fighters, and in doing so we defend France."

"As a young Catholic boy, I was no atheist like Sartre. The notion that man was born without purpose grated me, but I considered the words as I went to the cathedral with my mother. A visiting Cardinal, she said, and mildly curious I went along. As an altar boy I was assured of being able to see the fellow, and so I joined the procession of people who also had gone to meet him. It was an odd sight, lines of people queued up to knell at the feet of this fat man wearing gold and jewels, sitting in a chair." Alan's face changed, showing the utter disgust he had for that gross church creature.

"And then it was my turn. The man was clearly disinterested, and while he held out his hand for his ring to be kissed it was obvious his mind was elsewhere. And that is when it happened, right in my face I was presented with this enormous ruby that was set into the Episcopal ring, and I was expected to kiss it. Something turned in my stomach, some deep part of me was revolted in a way I cannot explain.

"All the privilege, the arrogance, the extraordinary falseness of the situation stood out like neon lights. This man was so proud, so rich, and so utterly uncaring that it repulsed me. This man, this church, it only existed because the poor gave it wealth and power. They were no better than the Fascists in Spain. I left that cathedral an atheist, and soon after, plagued by guilt or my conscious, I can't be sure which, I went with a few other boys over the Pyrenees.

"For the first time in my life, I was taken seriously and trained to be part of the resistance. I was not alone, many other boys of my age or not much more also heard this call. I can't even recall if I had permission to leave, I can't imagine I did. But at that time teenagers would be away all the time, Europe gave its youth so much more freedom than the Americans.

"We went to Leon and met Giron, the leader of the Marquis in that part of Spain. He organized for we boys to be properly trained, specifically in guerrilla tactics. Making explosives, destroying train lines and bridges. He did not send us into any sort of direct confrontation. Why? Not just because we were still boys, but because, as boys, we were good at disappearing. We did the deliveries, moved explosives, and generally helped the men create havoc.

"No-one was looking for wandering teenagers. We had enormous fun, it was a huge adventure, and I traveled back and forth between France and Spain many times before the main war started." He paused, took a sip of water, and laid back. Tracking down the path of the years, he began recalling the little details.

"This was the Maquis. As you know, they were the starting point for the French Resistance. So much of my life story was forged from these connections made in those early days as a child. Sartre was right in one sense, we make our purpose, but at the same time I cannot help but wonder how much of myself was made to fit my purpose. How much of this is destiny, and how much was my choice?

"Prior to 1939 and the onset of the War, my father came back from Berlin. There was an architectural commission he was looking at that took him there, and here saw first hand the hysteria. He was present during the Kristallnacht (crystal night) pogroms and saw first hand the madness and hatred that was taking over the German people. He knew war was coming, so as soon as he could arrange it, he shipped your grandmother and all of us out of France and back to New York. Back here, Big Cy (The family name for the grandfather) wanted me to undertake architecture, and I obliged the entrance exams and even passed, but to his dismay, I eventually chose to study fine arts back in Manhattan.

"Who knew at that age what an awareness for our future purpose for being might be, but I knew in my bones that my Raison D'etre did not lay in designing houses. I was the man making the knife, but completely unaware of the fact because I was blinded by ideals and notions of importance. I knew I wasn't an architect though.

" I also knew I wasn't a good Catholic, not just because of the Cardinals ring, but because before I reached New York I had already killed my first man. And what's more, I had absolutely no regret over this action."

Cyrus interrupted, "Was that the Filing Cabinet story?"

"I have told you that story many times."Alan laughs, "But let me tell you once more how it came about."

Note: Between 1936 and 1939 some 40,000 teenagers crossed the Pyrenees, from France into Spain, and involved themselves to some degree in the Spanish Civil War

Imagination is not an empirical or superadded power of consciousness, it is the whole of consciousness as it realizes its freedom.
Jean-Paul Sartre

The Filing Cabinet

The First Sign of Collaboration

It was early in 1939. Tension was everywhere. Those who understood what was happening knew war was on the doorstep. Czechoslovakia had been annexed and Europe was coming up to the start of the "false" war, the period where the West had declared because Hitler invaded Poland, but did nothing about it." Alan continued his tale:

"We had all heard of Crystal Night, my father had been there, in Berlin as it happened. Anyone with an ounce of sense knew that Germany was getting ready for war. My father was making preparations for us to move back to the States, and I went to one of the local cells in Orleans to explain what was happening. Here they recruited me for one last mission before I left France.

"The earliest form of what would become Vichy Government in the South had made excursions to see Hitler, making appeasement talks, and they were already rounding up the names of Jews. They would not oppose Hitler but welcome him. Why? He had ended the depression in Germany, and the country was brimming with confidence. Many in France dreamed of a new day and accepted that Hitler was bringing it.

"The Maquis wanted more information, even at this early stage, about these people. Because we were invisible, boys were often sent to gather information. We were teenagers wandering about, it was so normal no one paid us any attention. And so I was sent to a small camp outside of Orleans, to see what it was up to. To my surprise, the place was run by police, and as there was almost no security I was able to walk into one of the offices and open a filing cabinet.

"In there I found lists of all the local Jews. Father had already spoken of how the Germans were systematically rounding up and imprisoning these people, but what were the French police doing? I had a vial of hydrochloric acid for destroying documents, so I poured that over everything, but as I did so a large man, clearly not French nor a policeman, came in and spoke angrily in German.

"I knew my life was in danger, I could feel his hatred and then I saw his knife. I went to run but he knocked me over, thumping me with his leather bound fist. His other hand lifted up and was about to plunge in the dagger. I was already fading from consciousness, but I managed to punch him with the ring that had the poison needle. This was standard for Marquis because if you were searched it looked like you had no weapons.

When I awoke, I was badly bruised, but the knife had missed its mark. The German was slumped over me, and I had to push him off. He was dead. I can't say if it was the ring or the other boy I had with me. He was already gone, but I got out of there without anyone else walking in. And when I reported back, I was the only one to do so.

"Much was made of the report, I was asked over and over for the details. I was asked again and again about the documents, but it seemed the story checked out. The police were already working with the Germans in a covert collection of information about French Jews. And all this before they had even invaded!

"I never knew what became of that place, or what its purpose was, nor who the German was that I killed. Within weeks the whole family was on board the lle De France, the last passenger ship to leave France before the invasion of Poland. (when war was officially declared)

"The man running the Maquisard in that area was only a few years older than me, Jacques was his name. He said words to me as I left, words that stayed with me my entire life. *'It is one thing for the German to die. He deserved it, a filthy spy. But what of the others that helped him? They are worse because they CHOOSE their course. We all know why they are compiling lists, so they are as guilty as the German. They choose to cause their own countrymen suffering, and have abrogated their right to live in France'.*

"He was a fierce man, or so he seemed at the time. Hardened by his years in the Spanish Civil War, he knew what atrocities men could commit. The Nazi were there, you know, helping Franco. And then he continued, looking me firmly in the eye as he spoke. *'It is here we must kill our own people, and it must be done quietly. However, the message must also be sent, so we will have their throats cut, silently, in their own beds. No one but their guilty friends will see the pattern, and because of this, they will understand fear. They will know that they are known and will live in the certain knowledge that they will pay for their actions'.* At the time I thought this would be the last I would see of the Maquis, and Jacques, as I was about to head to New York. But I was wrong. When I returned as a serviceman with the 603d during the war, we found each other again."

(There is a noise of tires on gravel) "I hear your mother and sister have returned. Go get all the hugs and kisses from the women, Little Cy, but come back and talk with me more."

The Prodigal Son

The Family Reunited

The black car had parked and the passengers were bringing out bags of food and supplies. "My boy!" Cyrus' mother sees her son standing there as she gets out of the car. She holds out her arms and welcomes him with a kiss. "We went down to the bus station to find you, but here you are already. So good to see you."

"I haven't been gone very long, you know," he said as he was being smothered.

"But you are here, and this is what matters. Have you seen your father? Yes? Of course, you have. Let's get all this in and we can have a wine, would you like a wine? Of course, you would. Father will always have one at this time of day."

Annabelle Wood-Thomas had been married to Alan more than half her life. She was a teenager when they met, during the war years. She had been a live model, a nude model, in a school where he was studying art. She had been called "Dot", short for Dorothy, but Alan had given her a new name, Annabelle, and it stuck.

They had been married in February 1942, not long after America had become involved in the war. Alan had tried to join up earlier, but he had flat feet, and bad teeth, and had been rejected. But now all of this was to change. Word had also gotten out that the military was looking for people with an aptitude for art, and so he applied and was successful this time. Both he and his brother got in, and both were itching to get to Europe and give the Nazi a little of what they deserved.

But there was a problem. Alan's tests showed him to be suited for a role as a mechanic, and he was drafted into that battalion. It meant he had to do an extraordinary thing: In order to get to the 603d where he felt he needed to be, he had to incapacitate himself and make it so he would be unable to ship out.

Cyrus was thinking of all of this as his mother and he went back to "The Kings" room, as they referred to Alan. "The King" was chatty and with little prompting Cyrus got him focussed. What the son wanted to know more about was the early years, and in particular, re-hearing how he got into the special unit, written about in "Secret Soldiers" by Philip Gerard.

"Tell me again how you got into the 603rd Engineer Camouflage Battalion, father." Cyrus started after they had settled down. His dad was weak, and keeping him focused on the past would help, plus it was such an interesting story.

"Ah, you mean how I got out of the mechanic's battalion and into camouflage? Well, we know the story, how I got your poor mother here to pour the boiling water over my foot so I would be medically unfit to ship out. She almost passed out, but it got me the weeks delay I needed to transfer to the newly formed unit.

"I managed to get my brother in there as well, all by doing a few sketches for the Colonel in charge of the unit. All I knew was that I had to be in that unit, and by proving my capacity as an artist I got his ear. The rest as you know is history."

"Even before we got to France I was developing the inflatable tanks and a few other tricks to fool the Germans. I even had my own car and driver and was already a corporal by this time. But it was in France that this new world became exciting.

"Of course, as I spoke the language, HQ had many uses for me, and I was able to have things happen so much more easily than the usual non-com. And because I had personal friends in the resistance, this, along with my fluent French, meant that we could be truly effective. We had the Germans believing tank battalions were going through passes, and artillery was being mobilized in front to their left, and generally made it impossible for them to form a force of focus on any one assault that appeared to be coming at them.

"As you know, I was never one for drinking over much. A wine occasionally, but the boys with me were away from home and out to enjoy themselves. And so Gilles (his brother) and I had ourselves a good time sketching them as they got drunk and whored around.

"And then came that night when we were being mobilized, the lads with me were all drunk and sleeping in the back of the truck as we moved out. I don't know what woke me up, but something did. I looked up and out from the canvas covering us and saw the truck coming right at us. It was a transport taking a broken tank back for repair. I realized it was taking up most of the road, then I further realized we were going to hit it.

"To this day, I don't know how I managed it but I got off the back of that truck and into the snow beside the road just before the two transports hit. Everyone died, but I lived. Frozen, I made my way back to camp, back to making more inflatable tanks. It makes you wonder about fate."

Annabelle left the room. She knew the story so well, but this was a time for father and son. She went to prepare the evening meal, and Little Cy, as he was known in the family, realized that his father's thick French accent had once more faded, but only when he spoke to him alone.

"Did you know, Dad, that when you speak to others, you have a thick French accent, even with Annabelle. But with me, you drop it. Why is that?"

Finally, the boy was starting to see. The father laughed, and said, "I like to make sure everyone understands that while I am a proud American, my heart is French." Then he looks directly at his son, saying, "Everything I did in my life, everything, was based on my love of France. She is the heart and soul of my being, and the source of my inspiration. I want people to know and remember me as a French man living in America, not an American who spoke French."

Then Alan changed tact and went in a new direction. "One of the greatest moments of my life was meeting my spiritual father, Picasso. Yes, it was because of my role in camouflage, and being able to speak French, that I could organize it, and I remain grateful to America for all it has done for me and my family, but my heart is, was and always will be French. You know this, I don't have to remind you. The others, I like to constantly remind them what I am and where I came from. Plus, the French accent is good for business."

They both laugh, but a thought occurs to Cyrus, "There is something I am not clear on, this trip you took into Paris before it was liberated, to see Picasso, with who was it? Flemer? I mean, this never made a lot of sense to me and you have never explained what it was about. I found it difficult to imagine you both would risk being shot as spies just to go see Picasso or your grandparents."

Alan grows quiet. "It is something that was classified but I don't suppose it matters now." He paused and considered what he was about to say. "As you know, Hitler had given orders for Paris to be destroyed. As a result, my friends in the Maquis were anxious, yet at the same time, their informants told them that Von Choltitz wanted out. Ostensibly, the arrangement was for me to go to Paris to meet Picasso at the Hôtel de Savoie on the Rue des Grands Augustins, in the 6th. But you are wondering, how did I managed all this, being AWOL, getting a car, and actually getting into occupied Paris? It is one of my proudest secrets."

Alan laughs out loud, smiling at the madness of his youth. "Let me tell you the real reason I was in Paris with Flemer."

EXTRACT: "Secret Soldiers", Page 74: *"They also learned silk-screening techniques to create signs and posters. Flemer and his buddy, Alan Wood-Thomas, invented canvas-and-wood decoys of trucks, tanks and howitzers."*

Untold Secrets

Liberation Plans for Paris

EXTRACT: "Secret Soldiers", Page 189: "Wood-Thomas was more French than American. If you were told to pick out the Frenchman in a photo of the 603d, your eye would be immediately drawn to the slight, fair haired young man with the loose European posture."

The faded blue eyes traveled back to a far distant time. Alan in 1944 was a slender, blonde haired and remarkably fit young man, fighting in the 603d camouflage division. He had been integral in sorting out the issues and solving problems in the creation of the rubber tanks and other "fake" machinery to fool the Germans into believing there were armies where there were none. The crossing into Germany was largely made possible by the subterfuge of the 603d that led the Germans into believing an enormous army was present at the point they counter-attacked, now known as the "Battle of the Bulge".

Shortly before the surrender of Paris, Alan was stationed at Torce' en Charni. Under Col Reeder, the despised leader of the 603d, the non-fighting battalion had 'liberated' their one and only French town, and the people were ecstatic. (Described in 'Secret Soldiers' Page 186) Reeder gives a speech, written by Fred Fox and translated into French by Alan, ending with 'Viva La France!'.

The US military band strikes up 'La Marseillaise', the first time the national anthem has been heard in years, and there is rapturous applause. Tears, hugs, kisses, and the US soldiers are handing out sweets and chocolate. It was a classic scene that you see in the movies, played out in real life. The men are starting to feel like true liberators.

But clandestine meetings with the Maquis have brought up a very serious matter. The German General running Paris has been given orders to blow the entire city up, and to fight to the last man should the Allies invade. However, the information the Resistance has, via the Swedish Consul, was that Von Choltitz was wanting to cut a deal. He will surrender Paris, but only if his family can be extracted from Germany, and he is not to be tried for war crimes. *("Is Paris Burning" - Von Choltitz Biography)*

There was little point bringing the matter up with Reeder. The man had precious little imagination for war and no patience for the ideas given him by the unruly artists under his command. He wanted to be running a 'real' battalion, a proper fighting one, and felt his role in the 603d demeaned him.

All this was the story Cyrus already knew and had heard many times at Christmas or family gatherings. Now his father launched into the untold part of the story.

Alan began his tale. "As part of my role as a negotiator between the Allies and the French Resistance, I had a jeep and was able to travel without specific permissions for every journey. In this, I was to meet the great man himself, De Gaulle. He knew many of the Maquis that I was familiar with. That is when the overall plan for the liberation of Paris was outlined.

"I was not a party to the negotiations, but it was well known that Eisenhower was not interested in taking Paris. He knew it could end up like a Stalingrad and he did not want to focus the war effort in a drawn out campaign that had no military significance. But for the French, Paris was heart and Soul, the central goal and primary purpose. De Gaulle wanted Paris, but more importantly, he also knew 25,000 communists were in the city, ready to cause grief and mayhem against the Germans.

"It was not just the political advantage of getting in before this happened, Von Choltitz as the Befehlshaber, fortress commander, of Paris had been ordered to 'stamp out without pity' all civilian acts of disobedience or terrorism. This meant enormous destruction inside Paris would be inevitable. Many would die, buildings would be destroyed, and who knows how long it would go on for. But based on the information from my old friend from the resistance, Jacques, the German Commander knew there was no possibility of winning, and wanted a better solution.

"He wanted out. He had met Hitler before taking up his post and realized the man had gone mad. But he also knew that if he surrendered Paris, his family would be killed. The door was open if De Gaulle could get his family out, and if Eisenhower would guarantee he would not be tried for war crimes, a deal could be made. This required a coordinated effort, and the German wanted PROOF that the Allies had agreed, not just taking the word of some French resistance fighters.

"Before we saw De Gaulle, Jacques had shown me the cufflinks of the German Commander. He wanted to exchange these for one of the great French General's and one of Eisenhower's, as a clear imprimatur proof that both men had agreed in principle to the plan. Well, we did a lot of driving over the next few days, and I got to meet Eisenhower's Chief of Staff personally. He gave me a cufflink from the boss and ordered me to personally go into Paris and negotiate a surrender, if possible. But in no way was I to involve the US military in any active engagement. It was a matter between the Germans and the French.

"Nothing in writing, of course. A US military commander did not have the power to determine how a court after the war would deal with things, but the general outline, as per Von Choltitz's requests, was agreed to in principle.

"And so Flemer and I went forward. I had no official permission from Reeder or the 603d, but it was agreed at HQ I could take another French speaker, which was Flemer. If I got sick, or something happened, I would be able to confide in him what needed to be done. As it stood, he never knew anything other than it was a marvelous joy ride into enemy-held Paris."

Note: *There is little to no official documentation of one of the most significant events of World War Two, the Surrender of Paris. However, the run by Alan Wood-Thomas into Occupied Paris is a documented fact, as is the fact that he went there with the Maquis, the French Underground. It lends credence to the notion he was part of the negotiations.*

Example of Tank Decoy used by the 603d

Nazi Occupied Paris

Negotiations for Paris

EXTRACT: "Secret Soldiers", Page 190: *"Alan Wood-Thomas still had grandparents and friends in Paris, and he had close ties with the Maquis, the French Resistance. He and Flemer, who also spoke French, changed into civilian clothes. They rendezvous with friends of Alan Wood-Thomas, who picked them up in a Gazogene car that had been converted to burn charcoal instead of gasoline, and ingenious French contraption necessitated by the gasoline shortage."*

Alan looked weary, and Cyrus wondered if he had talked enough for the day. The Moon had risen, full and clear, and the stars gazed down. A scene of great beauty, the rustling of the wind in the reeds of the nearby river, the pensive light cast across the un-mown lawn, the moment stretching wide and open, like a lover welcoming you.

His father drank some water and propped himself up in his bed to continue the story. "The plan was very simple. Jacques and I were to meet Picasso at the Hôtel de Savoie, where he lived. In secret, the Swedish Consul, Raoul Nordling, would meet up with us. We had reasonable security in that it was not uncommon for Picasso to meet people, plus Von Choltitz had made sure his own men were stationed there that day.

"Nordling was extremely tense, but after I gave him the cufflinks from Eisenhower and De Gaulle he visibly relaxed, and explained in detail what was needed. Picasso himself was not present and was having coffee in another room, but just seeing him was a great joy. He was a true patriot and risked his life for this meeting to occur. A lot was riding on what happened next. Paris would become a hell-pit if we failed.

"In short, Von Choltitz wanted guarantees of his family being safe, not unreasonable, and in the confusion of Germany at that time there were many there who wanted to curry favor with the Allies. He himself would organize for them to get out of where they were being held, and it was then that they were to be collected. He also had another demand, a far more difficult one. He stipulated that the Allies had to take Paris, not the French. We all knew what would happen to him if the French forces came in.

"This was where the greatest risk lay. It was an impossibility to have Eisenhower to agree to head the charge into Paris, nor would De Gaulle agree to the Americans or British saving the French capitol. When Nordling was done, he said that the General's representative was waiting in the bar.

"We needed to meet his negotiator. There was nothing for it, we had to come face to face with a Nazi officer, and hope we lived. Explaining that it was not possible for the Allies to enter Paris was extremely difficult, but Jacques already knew this would be an issue. He offered a compromise, and explained that there was an armored battalion run by a French Captain, but manned purely by Spanish fighters, ex-civil war men. They had no particular ax to grind. Was this option an acceptable compromise?

"The man sent off a sachet to the General, listing all the terms and principles, and there were a good two hours of waiting where we did not know if we would live or die. Obviously, the Consul was gone, Picasso was no longer involved, and so we just sat there like turds on a rock." Alan paused his tale and looked at his son, "Unless you have felt the truly evil presence of the Nazi, the arrogance, the utter carelessness they held towards you living or dying, then you could never understand how even two hours of small chat by this adjudicate would curl your hair.

"The man was pure malice, yet so pleasant, so controlled. If the word came back the arrangements were unacceptable, we would have been shot, there and then. And he would not have given it a moments thought. But as he talked, I started to see the cracks appearing. We could not speak of our military arrangements, but he knew where every battalion was, where every commander was based, and he made a point of asking us if we knew of Hitler's latest invention, the newly drafted Sippenhaft law.

"Of course we had no idea, and he explained that now every commander on every front, as a result of the failed bomb plot where Rommel himself was implicated, had their families held as virtual prisoners, hostages to make sure the Germany Army obeyed Hitler's instructions. He was painting the picture for us very clearly, and in his way emphasizing that his commander wanted out.

"He did not introduce himself, but he had the green field patch of a staff officer and the insignia of Oberst. He was a Colonel, directly under the General. This was enough to make sure we understood that Von Choltitz was not alone in this decision.

"Jacques was nervous, though he did not show it. If this went wrong they would have presumed he was a Resistance fighter, and it was no bullet for him, but a slow torture. Finally, it came back, the general framework of a surrender. There can be no French army, the "La Nueve" Jacques had offered as a compromise was acceptable. But the details were very unclear. What made things even more complicated was the presence of the "werewolves" ... A new breed of German fanatic prepared to die for the Nazi cause.

"However, an agreement in principle was reached that Jacques knew would be workable with De Gaulle, and if Eisenhower agreed, a code word was to be sent out by the BBC in three days. Once this was announced, Von Choltitz would get his family out of where they were being held. They were to be collected, and the Spanish Unit could attack. The fanatics would not surrender, they would have to die, but the city administration would be in one location. Once the French force got there, the surrender could be signed. In this circumstance, he would not commence the destruction of Paris, as ordered.

"We had no idea how this would work, but it was early August already. The Allied forces were routing the German Army at every turn, and no doubt the city officers were all wanting to avoid a prolonged guerrilla war in a city where they were trapped. The worst outcome was the Communists seizing power, and with 25,000 of them in Paris, they had the greater numbers. All Germans would be summarily executed should that lot manage to gain control.

"In short, for the Nazi administration this was the best deal they would get. If you surrendered Paris and flew out to Germany, you and your family died. Blow up Paris, and you die gloriously, but this meant you were forever cursed in the history books, plus you were dead. If the Communists take over, you are dead. If the French march in, you are dead. Eisenhower, by refusing to take Paris had forced the General's hand, and so he had to make the deal, hoping for the best that he and his higher command would survive.

"I took the information back, along with another gift, an insignia from Von Choltitz's own uniform. And the rest, as you know was history. But after the liberation of Paris, I returned, to make a proper visit to Picasso."

EXTRACT: www.thedailybeast.com/who-liberated-paris-in-august-1944

"The Spanish detachment of the Free French Army, also known as "la Nueve" (from the French neuvième régiment), wore U.S. military gear, and drove U.S. tanks decorated with the Gaullist Cross of Lorraine, but they proudly carried as well such names as "Guadalajara," "Ebro," and "Teruel," sites of grand battles during their own cruel war. The "Nueve" was representative of the quite heterogeneous forces that retook the city."

Meeting Picasso

Picasso and the Resistance

Alan looked into the distance, remembering that day in 1944, just as the US army was making ready to push the Germans out of France. "Finding Picasso after the surrender of Paris was not hard. In the liberated city, he was now able to move about. He was no longer the 'corrupt' person living under the Nazi, and he was welcomed everywhere as one of the true French men who never gave in to the German oppression.

"I only met him this one other time, not at his hotel, but in his Montmartre studio," Alan reminisced. "I told him how grateful I was for the inspiration.

"But Picasso, he really impressed me. There was no complication in the man or his work, nothing but a simple purity. I took along a few samples of my own art. People had criticized my nudes, minimalist they eventually called it, but Picasso saw it right away. After this, what everyone else thought about my work meant nothing to me. He gave me the courage to be myself as an artist. Just a nod, it was the simplest sign he understood and approved. You cannot believe how much it meant to me.

"And then later, I began to realize it was not only the art he approved of. It was ME." Tears formed in Alan's eyes. "He approved of ME, the art, the person, the fact that as a child I worked against Franco. And of course, because the City of Light had been saved from the Germans."

"Paris after the liberation disturbed me, though. It was a frenzy, a madness. The people were not natural anymore, and I suspected it was due to a deep inner insecurity. They loved having the soldiers there, at first, but as we now know, in the months that followed, as the shortages continued, the people became bitter. (Alan laughs) As if having the Bosch there would have been better."

Alan stopped, his breathing shallow. Cyrus and he are the only ones in the room, and he leaned towards his son conspiratorially. "Jacques caught up with me after I met Picasso. He understood what our little secret group was up to. Yes, I know we were sworn to secrecy, but Jacques was central to our forces being able to connect to the resistance, and he had ways of knowing everything it seemed. The man offered the full support of the Maquis in helping set up and move into place our elaborate hoaxes. It was clear to him that confusing the enemy and making them distrust their intelligence was the quickest way to get them out of France. He then asked me if I remembered the filing cabinet incident before I left, which of course I did. My first dead German was not something I could forget.

"Well, it turned out that only a year prior to this meeting in Paris they found some German war records, and a photo of the man was there. This was an SS officer, in France, looking to find the soft points in the leadership. Proof of collaboration was seen by your willingness to gather lists of Jews and homosexuals, and there were many willing parties on our side to do this. Specifically the leadership of the police.

"During the war, executing a German meant reprisals where whole villages were killed. Innocent men women and children would be mowed down and buried in a ditch outside their town for the sole reason that a Maquis group was nearby. The evil bastards, but all through those years the resistance had been compiling a list, and Jacques said he was willing to share this if I would be willing to report the whereabouts of any persons on that long line of names that I discovered.

"I was happy to do so. And yes, I knew what would occur once I reported one of these people's location, but they deserved to die. And so my war in France was many sided, building and designing the tools to confuse the German intelligence, liaison with the French Resistance, translating and helping communications at HQ, and now it was also tracking down any collaborators and Nazi that escaped the net and slipped back into society.

"I already had my own jeep and driver, because I was always at HQ translating, and helping with communications in one way or another. I was made a sergeant and given a pretty free hand. With the resistance helping us, now I could coordinate activities between our military and their saboteurs. It was remarkably effective, and we made certain none of the Bosch rested easy at night. The German moral collapsed, and they fell back to their own borders within months of the fall of Paris.

"Did you know that the 603d fought on more fronts than any single unit in any division of any army within the Allied Forces? The resistance is what allowed us to do this. They found the open passes, the back roads, the way to smuggle in the fake tanks and airfields that forced the Germans to think we were where we were not, and which then meant they were caught by surprise when the actual attacks did arrive. *No single force did more to help end to the war in France than the 603d.*

"I retained my connection with Jacques and helped him track down some of the SS who had escaped the net and made their way back to Germany when we got there. This continued after the War, but very few of the Nazi came to the States. We were sent back home in June of 1945, though we were not demobilized until the Japanese surrender. And then, the strangest thing. I get accused of stealing classified equipment and got sent up for a court martial. This would have made future travel difficult, and then it struck me. If they take me to court, and they ask what I did, their secret army is no longer a secret.

"So I point this out, and they drop all charges. After this the other detail of recording my name as Mood, rather than Wood, caused more confusion but eventually, I got back home to your mother.

"Prior to the war I studied architecture for almost two years, but my heart was not in it, and I moved from Rhode Island and lived with my mother in New York. I did odd jobs, working as the elevator man at the Radio City Music Hall, whatever paid. Then I meet your mother, and we move in together. My sister then left the 89th Ave apartment, so that Annabelle and myself could live alone, or at least just with my Mamman. Annabelle then stayed on there during the war, with Mamman and her sister. After I got back, I started to supplement the family income doing drawings and teaching art to rich Jews at a resort owned by Bill Hahn.

"I suspect I got that job not just because I was a good artist, but because I helped track down the Nazi for the Resistance. Your sister was born within a year, which proves we were getting on!" (he laughs) "What can I say, the nudes I was doing of your mother were popular, and one thing leads to the next."

"And this is when it started happening."

"The visions?" asked Cyrus.

"Yes, the visions." Alan said, nodding.

If you are lonely when you're alone, you are in bad company

Jean-Paul Sartre

The Visions

The Psychic Nazi Hunter Awakes

Note from 'Little Cy' to the Author: My father came to America just before the war started. He was at Princeton, Rhode Island and studied with his father 'Big Cy' for 2 years before quitting architecture. (even though he had been admitted to the third year of architecture at Princeton) It was a great disappointment to "Big Cy".

He then moved to New York City and lived with his mother. Wanting to know more about his true love, which was art, he paid a dollar to draw a nude model in the art school. He was not studying there, he studied on his own. The model was my mother. (and voila, here I am today!)

After this he joined the American Army and did his thing in Europe with the 603d. The war ended, and he returned and worked at the Radio City Music Hall operating the elevator. The Rockette dancers used to change in the elevator and he would tantalize us little boys, telling saucy stories. He did other odd jobs, lived with my mother, and there Alan and Annabelle (Little Cy's mother) had their first girl Liane, and then another, Diane. This is when he spent two hours every night drawing my mother, teaching himself to draw the human form.

It was around 1948 that they decided to live a calmer life and move to Connecticut, eventually to the town of Clinton where Alan's mother's boyfriend Pierre Houpert lived. Before getting to Clinton (which is right next to Westbrook where he died) they lived in Branford for a year or two and spent a lot of time at the beach.

Pierre was a very simple man. He lived to 103 and we had dinner at his house almost every Sunday for more than a decade. Everybody there spoke French except for my mother and myself.

Pierre was a real character. He spat on a newspaper on the floor, smoked his pipe and played backgammon with his French neighbor. (who later shot himself for reasons unknown) While he was a jewelry designer, Pierre apparently never worked a day after he was 35 years old, having inherited a good amount of money, and after that played the stock market.

Alan's visions started at or around the time they were preparing to move from New York to Connecticut.

Little Cy looked over at his father. He appeared to be deep in contemplation, looking back to where the story started. When you are old, the past is but yesterday. There are no more dreams of things to come, there are only memories, and these are what define us. Alan gazed inwardly and began his tale. "I am not certain as to the exact date, but I remember the week itself as clearly as I can see my hands in front of me. For no apparent reason, other than feeling unreasonably tired, I would lay down, and then I would find myself flying high above a city.

"The first one started high over the continent of Europe. I was soaring in the sky, gazing down, I was in the clouds and decided to sweep down. There I saw beneath me what was clearly Italy, just over the top of the boot, off the coast of the Adriatic Sea. Between the heel of the boot and mainland Europe, I came in, at an extraordinary speed, noting as I did the incredible color and depth unfolding in front of me.

"It seemed that it was brighter than real life and more clear. I could see details with extraordinary detail. Though I had never visited, I recognized from the coastline that I was descending into Venice, the city of canals. I came in closer: Every detail, every house, the gondolas, they all were in perfect focus.

"At the edge of the city, near the southern end of the S-curve, I saw the famous Piazza San Marco, or St. Mark's Square in English. From the air, it was apparent that the structure was actually slightly trapezoidal. At the wide end of the square, I could pick out the five Byzantine domes on the roof of St. Mark's Basilica, forming the shape of a cross. Also at the wide end of the Piazza, slightly to the southwest, I recognized the red brick Campanile di San Marco, the Bell Tower of St. Mark's, the tallest structure in the city.

"The clarity of focus I possessed was so great that I could easily make out the patterned surface of the piazza, thick with pigeons and tourists in the bright daylight.

"Swooping close to the green-tiled spire of the bell tower, I saw the golden statue of the Archangel Gabriel at the top of the spire, rotating in the wind. I could even look into the bell tower itself to view the lone bell, all that was left of the original set of five bells, each of which had once chimed a different message.

"To the right of the Basilica, there was the U-shaped Palazzo Ducale, or Doge's Palace, with its two rows of delicate stone arches and patterned brickwork. After this I flew over the city itself, noticing the bright orange tile roofs of the buildings packed together like so many sardines, the canals full of gondolas, the bridges, and the narrow streets, some with lines of laundry strung across them from building to building.

"After this, I came back to physical awareness and sketched what I saw. At the time, I was familiar with some of the architectural landmarks, as my father had studied these. I imagine I had seen them in his library, but as to an overall view of the city, all I knew was that it was Venice. And so the next day I went straight to the New York public library and pulled out some research books.

"To my astonishment, everything I saw had been absolutely accurate. Even the smallest of details, such as the marks on the bell in the bell tower. It was all there, in pristine photographic perfection. This is what astonished me, I saw in absolute clarity things I have never seen before, things I didn't even know existed. I had sketched them after the vision, and here they were in the library books.

"I was shocked, and started looking up what they had in the library to explain this. And there were some books on dream travel, a few notes in Jung about the Cosmic Unconscious, about how some people were able to speak fluently in a language they had never heard under hypnosis. The closest thing seemed to be a what they called Lucid Dreaming.

"Then the second vision came, this time it was San Francisco. Again, I had never visited, but while I had seen photographs, in the vision I could see every bolt on the Golden Gate Bridge, I could read the toll signs on the motorway across it. I could even fly under the bridge and see the boats sailing beneath her. But this time I realized I must be dreaming. I realized also that there was no sound, only pristine color and an utterly clear three-dimensional perception of everything around me.

"I even started to enjoy it, sailing beside the sailboats, thinking how wonderful it must be to travel this way over water. I even went to reach down to touch the ocean, but then the alarm clock woke me. It was another working day, but before I left I very quickly did sketches of what I saw, as I wanted to verify later at the library as to how accurate the visions were.

"Once more, that afternoon I found photographic books on San Francisco, and they matched the vision exactly. Even the toll fare of fifty cents, the same font on the same size board, it was all there. It was so precise, so defined, that I have no doubt at all that I actually visited this place in my dream.

"Each night for seven nights, another city, and every one of them matched exactly what I saw in the library the next day. None of these cities had I been to, or studied, or knew anything about, yet I was able to sketch the architectural points of interest with complete clarity."

Alan paused, scratched his nose, drank some water, and rearranged his sitting position in bed. The sunlight was filtering in through the open doors, throwing patterns of light and shade across the room. "Of course, I mentioned all of this to Annabelle, and she suggested that maybe it was a sign to go back to architecture, as my father had always wanted. I had no idea, but in a chance meeting with Holmes (John Cellon Holmes - the man who coined the "Beat Generation" term) and Harrington (Alan Harrington - Later to write 'The Secret Swinger' and 'The White Rainbow') having coffee at a little Italian place on Carmine street, just off Bleeker.

"I mentioned these visions, and they seemed fascinated, especially when I pulled out the sketches. Harrington had lived in San Fran, and knew the details of what I drew. He was amazed and could not believe I had not been there in person. He invited Annabelle and myself back to his apartment for dinner that evening, where we also met Kerouac. I took with me a number of the 'travel' sketches, and though no one had any idea what it was about, they were all fascinated. Hiroshima, Chicago, London, Paris and Mexico, all places I had never seen, but where every time my sketches married up to the photos in the library.

" *'Maybe you are astrally traveling to the library in your dreams?'* Harrington suggested, which made everyone laugh. No one really understood it. All were convinced it was not a call to architecture though, but that the sketches were proof of my ability as an artist.

"Kerouac was the one who put the Eastern view on it, that I was a Soul, set free of the body, and able to travel at will. Regardless, this started off my long connection with the beat writers, who as you know would call into our house in Connecticut on a regular basis."

"You still have the sketches you did of those soiree's?" Cyrus asked.

"Yes, in the workroom. Your sister knows where." (Alan had converted the shed out back to a work room)

"Soon after this, the real visions started. I remember it clearly, October 1947, in Central Park, before we moved. I was sitting watching the birds when I faded out, and I saw with extraordinary clarity the town of Lyon from the air. I knew it had to be Lyon because I knew the geography, and it was very clearly France. You cannot miss the meeting of the Rhone and Saône Rivers.

"Once more I was like a bird, flying through the air, seeing every tiny detail. This time, however, I am drawn to a specific spot, a house on a hill. I see the neat lawn, the clean driveway, the old fashioned sash windows, lifted up to let in the autumn air. And then I am drawn INTO the house, I see the occupants, a wife, some children, and an old man, maybe sixty years of age.

"They are wealthy, as I can see servants, a maid, a cook. Only the very privileged had these things in post war France. I am an eye floating, invisible, observing everything. Then everything focussed on the owner of the house, a florid, round faced man who looked like a bad tempered Santa Clause without a beard. I could feel his moodiness, his anger. The mouth never smiled, and the gray hair was like wire.

"Then I see the family getting ready for bed, the servants all leave to go to their own homes, but the man goes to his own room, not his wife's. I see this clearly, and he falls asleep. Finally, I come back to myself, it is chilly in Central park, but I dash off a few sketches while it is fresh in my mind, noting the little things, like an ornament on his desk, a wall clock, the knobs on his bed. And the man's face, this is still perfectly clear in my mind's eye.

"After this I go home, wondering what it was about, but who knows. I have dinner, go to bed, but at some point in the early hours of the morning, I am back in Lyon, this time watching as the man gets about his mornings business. The fellow has breakfast, and ventures out into the street. I follow behind him as he moves into an open doorway that leads into a sort of tunnel, which in turn leads to a point some blocks from the man's home.

"It is a mill, and the man goes in, meets with the owner. This is another face I can vividly see and recall after I wake. I can see the high ceilings inside, and the place is clearly a textile mill. Then the man leaves and goes back into one of the tunnels that were nearby. My focus then falls on the detail of the odd path itself, specifically the brickwork that is clearly very old.

"I wake and sketch it all down, including the pattern of bricks I saw in the enclosed alleyway, as well as the other face, and the outside appearance of the mill that the man in there apparently owned. I do not know why, but I felt it was extremely important. This was the vision that started everything. I had no idea at the time, of course."

The evening was coming in, the cool days at the end of Summer were fading into Autumn, and the first of the leaves were beginning to turn. Cyrus said nothing, knowing his father would pick up the story when he felt too, but the old man fell asleep. The son feels a slight sense of urgency, but all in good time. He had to get a few things ready at any rate. Cyrus needed to find some work, and he was seeing a person about doing some house painting the following day. They were not wealthy and he needed to do something to help around the house with money.

He had not known until he returned how tight things had become. With his father unable to teach or work, they were relying on his sister and his mother's part time incomes. His Aunt was there, but with him home she no longer felt the need to stay. He reflected that night just how much his family had lived on a hand to mouth existence all their lives. It didn't seem to bother anyone, but it was hardly like some of his friends.

So many people had parents who owned several properties, had good pensions and lived in the security of knowing there was cash in the bank and plenty of assets. But his father's dedication to his visions and to his art meant he spent so much time away, and Cyrus never really understood how they made ends meet. But they did.

Old family friends were coming over that evening, to say hello to Cyrus, and see how Alan was doing. His mother had laid out a goodly proportion of the weekly budget to have a really nice meal for everyone. Roast beef, creamed cauliflower, potatoes, and peas: It hardly seemed like an extravagance to people now, but it was back then, and there was plenty of it.

When Alan woke he made his way out of his bed to sit with everyone, and smiled at the familiar scene replayed so often in his life. Out of the blue, he looked over to Little Cy (The family name for the grandfather was 'Big Cy', and the son, 'Little Cy') and said, "You know, it was a meal like this that kicked everything off. You remember your grandmother's friend, Pierre Houpert?" Then he coughed and asked to be taken back to his room.

After the meal was done Cyrus called by to find him still awake, ready to continue his tale.

If you want to deserve Hell, you need only stay in bed. The world is iniquity; if you accept it, you are an accomplice, if you change it you are an executioner.

Jean-Paul Sartre

Back to France

The Journey to Lyon

This last vision was different to the flying dreams where he saw the cities. Here, he did not seem to have the choice of where he wanted to go. It was more like he was being instructed to look at very specific things. And it left Alan feeling uncomfortable, not with the vision, it was still a matter of curiosity, but in the sense that he felt he had to DO something about it. But what?

It was Annabelle that suggested he write to his friend, Jacques, in Paris. After the war, Alan's former connection to the resistance did private investigation work. He had a tremendous amount of information from his days in the Maquis, and he could now use this to find people, lost property and items of value taken by the Nazi. It was usually the relatives of the deceased Jews that wished to have things tracked down. Alan had an address, which turned out to be his parent's house, so he wrote asking Jacques to get more details on this very specific and strange thing he had experienced.

Alan posted over the drawings, and the image of the man he had seen, with a note explaining he had no idea what it was about, but it seemed important. If Jacques could follow it up and just check if there was anything of value in this matter, it would allay his concerns. The visions were so detailed he could even record the man's name as he saw it on an envelope at the house and the details of the street address. Alan was surprised to receive a telegram back in under ten days. Jacques must have responded very soon after receiving the mailing.

Weirdly, it asked for him to come over to Paris, as the matter was important. As he settled back with a warm Cocoa, the father picked up from where he had left off earlier. "I admit to being surprised, and yet, in my bones, I felt I had to know if this vision was accurate. I don't know why, but it was under my skin, and I was very pleased when Jacques responded. However, I had very little money and could not let the family starve while I went on a wild goose chase overseas. And yet, despite reason opposing this, everything inside me shouted GO!"

"And at this time, another vision came. This time it was Switzerland, Zurich. An apartment in a small block where an aging man lived alone. The thing that really disconcerted me as I was 'flying like a bird' in the mans flat, was that the man had a framed picture of Adolph Hitler in his bedroom. The dream continued, and I watched him come home from work, and go straight out. He lived alone, and apparently spent most of his evenings at the local bar, drinking himself to oblivion.

"Carl Reimer was his name," Alan paused, and added, "Of course, I drew the man, his flat, the surrounding area up, and sent this as well off to Jacques. Ten days later, another telegram, insisting that I come to Paris immediately."

He paused and looked directly at Cyrus once more. "Do you remember I asked if you remembered Pierre Houpert earlier?"

Little Cy knew the man quite well. When his grandmother separated from his Grandfather, Monsieur Houpert was a regular visitor. He gathered the fellow had been in love with Violette (the grandmother) since Paris and apparently followed her over here when he discovered she was single once more. They never married, but he was often by her side, and his Grandfather was rarely in the same place with him. The family often had Sunday lunch at his house in Connecticut.

"Yes, of course. Big man, wealthy. I presume Mamman's boyfriend."

"Well, he was. He was also a financier and well connected with a lot of the old money in New York. At a family dinner party just like tonight, way back in 1947, he turned up at our house in New York. This was unusual because he generally did not involve himself in our family business. We would visit him every week, but he almost never came to see us. He seemed very interested in my visions and asked a lot of questions. I saw no problem with describing to him what happened, and he seemed fascinated by the entire process.

"At the time, I thought he had some religious interest and was perhaps a Rosicrucian, or similar. I had been reading up on what there was about traveling out of the body, and there were lectures by the Spiritualist Church on Dream Prophecy and the like. As you know, I have no interest at all in anything like this, but it seemed that he did, so after the meal, we went for a walk to a local coffee shop, and we talked in depth about the visions.

"In the end, he offered to pay my costs for going to Paris, which seemed very odd to me at the time. He said he wanted to do so, because my Mamman was worried about me, and felt I really should put this matter to rest. I declined the offer, but after this, he decided to buy some paintings, and I was given an invitation to Carlbach's Gallery. The man was focussed on ancient art, but he said he was developing a new clientele and was interested in stocking some of my work.

"It was not for public display, but even so, due to his extensive private clientele, I regularly had an income from that source. It was where I met Katzenbach, who you saw might recall visiting our family studio here in Connecticut? I only found out years later that both men were invested in finding a solution for the lost Jewish families and the repatriation of their losses from the war.

"But for the present, it meant that I had the funds to go to Paris, and with Annabelle's blessing, I went to see Jacques. To be honest, I knew something was up even then, but I had no idea where all of this was leading. I gather now that it was Jacques who contacted Pierre Houpert because he wanted to make sure I got over there.

"I arrive in Paris, and I am collected from the airport by Jacques, and he simply says that we are going directly to Lyon after I freshen up at his parents. I do so, have a meal, and that very night we are driving South to Lyon. We arrived in the early hours, and Jacques asks me if I thought I could find my way to the house I saw.

"Well, I am as curious as he is to find out, and so we go to a point where I get an overview of the town. In the morning light I make out the general shape of the hill where I saw the house, and so we go over to there. Then, I start to clearly remember the details and can point out the house. I am shocked because it is EXACTLY as I saw it in my vision.

"Then we travel back to where I saw the man walking through the tunnels, and to my surprise, there WERE tunnels, of a sort, right there in the town. I realize they were more like enclosed alleyways, really."

It's quite an undertaking to start loving somebody. You have to have energy, generosity, blindness. There is even a moment right at the start where you have to jump across an abyss: if you think about it you don't do it.

Jean-Paul Sartre

December 1947 - Lyon

Standing in the curious covered alleyways of Lyon, the French man explained what they were for. "They are called traboules, Alan," Jacques spoke as they inspected the passageways. "These were constructed in the 18th century by the masters of the silk trade here. They were built to protect the silk as it was moved from factory to storage, then to the wharves. These features are unique to this town and were used by the resistance to hide from the Nazi and the local Vichy Police. So let us check the specific ones you made the drawing of."

Alan and Jacques follow the path of his dream, and to Alan's surprise, everything was exactly as he saw it. Even the pattern of bricks he drew matched perfectly the drawing made of them in New York. So too did the mill appear in the same place as seen in the vision. Alan asks Jacques what this was all about. Why did he want him to come all the way to France, just to confirm the accuracy of the drawing that were sent?

It seemed that Jacques was finally ready to talk, and explain what this was all about. "Do you remember I gave you a list, during the war, when you were here with the 603d?"

"Of course, and I returned it before we left. What has this to do with the vision?" Alan asks.

"One of the names on that list now lives in the house you saw in the vision, and the other one you saw runs the mill the man from that house went to see. He had been considered for the list, but was not seen as being overly corrupt, and left off."

"Incroyable! what an extraordinary coincidence!" Alan is amazed.

"Is it? I thought so as well when I first realized this. But the real reason you are here is that when I saw the image you drew, I immediately remembered the face. This was a Vichy policeman who vanished, he was one who had slipped the net. His superior was caught, jailed, but out of nowhere, you send me a drawing of a man I had personally hunted, but could not find. Further research showed that BOTH men had made a profit out of trading souls to the Nazi for cash and privilege. Yet they were both living here, wealthy, content, and free. Right here in Lyon."

Jacques sucked in the cold, dawn air through his teeth. He had so much to say and was gathering his words, to make sure everything was crystal clear. "I hope you grasp this, I was LOOKING for this man, and I have vast tools at my disposal to find people. But I could not find him until your drawing came through.

"The one at the house, the one whose'name you saw was Trudeau: That is not his real name. It is Taussard, the second in charge of Police in Vichy during the war. The man who owns the mill? Rene' Dubois. He did not change his name. He was a minor collaborator with the Nazi, but until your drawing turned up, he was not a name of great importance to us. Like so many businessmen in that period, they gave over the Jewish workers to the Gestapo. But now I start to look deeper, and it seems that he used the war as an opportunity to get rid of opposition. Of course, many of the textile mill operators here were Jewish. And it goes much deeper. Du Bois did not just hand over Jewish names, as we had thought, now we look deeper we find that his name turns up as a guarantor for shipping charges on sending those Souls to the death camps.

"People seemed to think that the Nazi just shipped people where they wanted, but this is only a small part of the story. People had to be paid, shipping companies still charged money, but the Nazi would not cover these costs and forced local communities to pay. Those who guaranteed payment were placed into a favored position, and Du Bois was one of these. These men FINANCED the Jews and others being sent to slaughter.

"And it gets more curious. Taussard had known Dubois for many years, it seems they worked together during the war on one of the worst crimes, the imprisonment of the children at Vél' d'Hiv? It is still one of the worst excesses of the Vichy Government, and one of the strangest events of the war, where the children of Jews, specifically children the Nazi had not even asked for, were imprisoned to basically starve or freeze while their parents were sent off to labor camps.

"These scum took it upon themselves to round up everyone, even the children, and eventually send them to their deaths. They knew there were no labor camps. These men were fully aware of what fate was to fall on the heads of those they shipped out.

"And as I look at this, voila! The missing pieces start to fit together. Dubois was the man responsible for sending the Jews that owned this house where Taussard now lives to Auschwitz. He took their looms, their business contacts, their client lists, and their best non-Jewish workers. He made a lot of money off the backs of those he condemned, but as the war turned and Paris was liberated the rats went into hiding. The former owners were called Trudeau, so Taussard now calls himself Trudeau and moves his family into the house of those dead Jews, while Dubois vouches for him as a returning relative. Because of this action, the home never made it onto the repatriation lists.

"If a relative asks about a property like this, they are told the matter has been settled, and the closest relatives have been moved in. A small risk for a huge gain.

"To confirm this, I accessed the German records, and Du Bois' photo is there, alongside a ledger that showed he underwrote the costs of shifting the Jews from Lyon to Drancy for the Vichy Government." (The Vichy

Government not only had to pay the German soldiers wages but also all the costs of running the war in Germany. The transportation of Jews to labor and death camps was charged out to the government. Private citizens underwrote specific charges in return for favorable treatment.)

"Can you imagine two more guilty people?" Jacques stated the question as if it were a fact.

"I agree, they are guilty." Alan echoed.

"Guilty." A third voice behind them spoke.

"Welcome Number Three. I am very glad you were on time. You have everything you will need?" The third man, who Alan did not know, simply nodded. "You must have both done before morning. I put the address of the mill owner in your equipment, yes?" (The man nods again) "You have taken care of the dog?"

"As instructed," the fellow finally speaks, clearly a Southern French accent.

"Report back in Paris. We will leave directly." Jacques ushers Alan back to the car. "Do you have a concern with this, Number One?"

"No Number Two, none." Alan recognized Maquis business when he saw it. No names, just numbers. Of course, 'Jacques' was also not the real name of the man before him, either. No one knew his name, though he knew everyone else's. Regardless, collaborators of such vindictive and callous natures had only one fate, death.

"Good, well the next step is to find who should be the rightful owners of the house. I will put in a report to people I know. They will research the remaining family of the people who lost their mill and property and hand these back to the closest relative. This is what I really do Number One. I call it balancing the books."

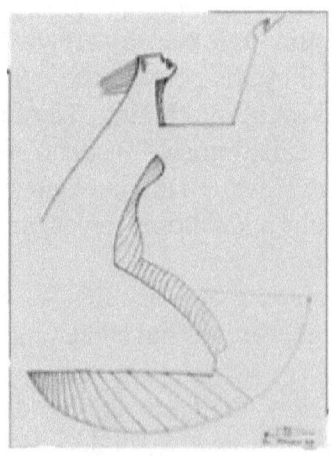

Return to Paris

It had been a very long day, and Alan and Jacques retired to a private hotel on the outskirts of Paris. Jacques said they need not worry about the bill, as the owner was an ex-Maquisard and they were on official business.

There in the early hours, they got some sleep. When Alan woke in the morning it was to the smell of croissants and fresh coffee. Mon Dieu! The things he missed living away. "The second vision you had, I have had this checked out as well. Are you interested?" Jacques was sitting sipping a black coffee at the French windows, gazing out over the countryside.

"I am to presume it was another collaborator, and this is why you wanted me here, yes?" Allan responded.

"Yes, it is so. But it is no collaborator this time, it would seem that in some manner you found a genuine Obersturmführer from the SS, hiding in open sight. This package was waiting for me when we came here last night."

Jacques let Alan see a file that had been delivered to the hotel. It would seem that the photo in the official German record was clearly the man he had seen in his vision. Obersturmführer Otto Reimer was listed as one of the "missing" members of the SS who had fled from Germany before the Nazi surrendered. He had been a commandant of a work camp in Austria called Ebensee. The name Alan had seen on a letterbox was Felix Reimer, so the man in Zurich had apparently felt so safe he merely changed his first name.

"This particular German officer ran a work camp, but he was a sadist. He beat men to death, starved them and when they died, he took anything they owned, including their gold teeth if they had fillings. He was known and feared for his unmitigated cruelty but was much awarded by his commandant because he got things down.

"He is now the superintendent at a local factory, has virtually no friends, and from recent observation keeps very much to himself. I have an operative who lives in the area collecting more details on the man, but the proof is right here. (he taps the file) You have found another one. And this one was as cruel as the very worst of the Nazi. He would have been one of the few who would have been punished if he had been caught. But, like so many of them, he had escaped."

Jacques paused, pulled out a Gauloise and lit up, breathing out a plume of smoke that spills over the streams of morning sunlight that pour into the room. "The question is, does this continue? Will there be more, visions, as you call them? I must let you know fully my interest in this matter. Yes, I am a private investigator, but not the usual 'find out if the wife is having an affair' sort of man. I have been employed by wealthy Jewish families, who know of my association with the Maquis.

"I am contracted to find their lost property and to put applications in to the relevant government agencies on their behalf. Real estate, art, jewelry, pretty much anything of value which was taken by the Germans. I track all this down for them. Based on results, they pay me extremely well. Often I find situations just as your first vision outlined, a Nazi or a collaborator who worked the system at the end of the war to ingratiate their own pocket and did so at the expense of some Jewish family that they had killed or had removed, though either amounts to the same thing.

"If I find such a situation, I resolve it. There are members of the political elite that consider it a good will gesture. While neither I nor any of my associates, such as Number Three who you met, will take money for eliminating these scum, my organization does accept the covering of the physical costs in such missions. And there are many expenses: fares, lodging, etc.

"All involved are people I have known since the Spanish Civil War. In the case of Number Three, It was his job back then, and he does it today as a matter of honor. And so it remains, that for no pay, he removes the vermin from the gutters. Of course, he does not suffer for his service to France, and as long as he follows protocols, he is relatively safe. From my end, I know many high-up members of our Police who understand what has happened. As long as there is clear evidence, which is provided through discreet channels, investigations are limited. We must be careful, of course, but for our part, we merely continue the unfinished work we did through the war.

"Obviously, there are stringent measures in place to assure we have the right target. We have access to the German records, and the resistance files, and many other files as well. We are of mutual benefit to others who have the same goal, which is removing the last of the Nazi from this planet. But no-one, and I stress no-one, has ever been able to give me such complete files on secret Nazis as what you have provided."

Jacques got up and walked across the room to where Alan was pouring his coffee. "I know you, Alan Wood-Thomas. I know your history since you met Sartre, and when, in the course of the war, you joined the 603d I considered it fate. It is why we in the resistance were so happy to work with you. You now understand it was no coincidence I was there when you met Picasso. I have been a shadow in the background, helping you to help France. But these visions you have, what I do not understand is HOW. How are you able to find these people that no-one has been able to find."

Alan stopped and stared at the man. "I thought I made it perfectly clear. I am not doing this, it just comes to me. I do not ask for it, I do not look for it. I do not even know if it will continue."

Jacques just grunted. "Well, if it does, we need to develop a way to communicate that is not via the mails or telephone. We have certain protections in place through our connections, but this is no guarantee. De Gaulle has started to crack down on the vigilante groups, and the French authorities are looking at people taking revenge against collaborators, and making an example of them. So we must develop a set of codes similar to what we used in the resistance.

"Clearly, things are more difficult with you living in New York, but if you do have more of these visions you must never contact me directly again. We must never again be seen together in France.

"Now as fortune will have it, most of my business is now coming from the States, and friends there have offered me an office to conduct interviews with clients. So before you travel back home to your lovely wife and girls, let us put in place a simple set of instructions that keep everyone safe."

And so they set out the protocols for communication, the codes to be used, and the framework under which this would all happen. It was nothing new. The Maquis had always used public libraries to send and receive messages. Reference books never left the library and were rarely looked at, and so they were the perfect connection point between the artist and the person gathering the information.

When a vision occurred Alan would sketch all the details and put them into a package that would be hidden about town. The details of where to find the information would be likewise written in code on a postcard of the Eiffel Tower. This would be left in a prearranged book.

As the post card was placed, a note was to be sent to Jacques' office, as if it was a client asking for information. *'I need the location of the butcher shop in Nice'* would be code for looking up a particular atlas where Nice could be found in the maps. When someone went to collect this a coded message was there. If it were a postcard it meant a vision had occurred, and a simple code on the back would indicate the need to meet in a specific park at a particular time in order to exchange the package with the drawings of the scene. The postcard would be blank apart from a simple message that was code for the arrangements.

Or it could be *'What is the history of Napoleon in Paris in 1813?'* which meant the reference book on the Napoleonic wars would have a postcard marking the chapter on 1813. Once more, a simple code would reference a park or a train station where a package could be exchanged.

Once Jacques' staff in New York had the package, it was simply broken up into sections, and forwarded on to him using separate couriers, along with a large amount of other paper work that came in from clients. No name or drawing of a face ever went together with an address, and every item of importance simply had another postcard attached. In this manner, each vision reached the Paris office in a manner that was impossible to track, even if some official happened to look through any particular courier parcel.

But they never did. Paperwork was not something customs officials were interested in, and couriers were almost never searched. What was not known to Alan or Jacques in those early days was just how often a vision would come, and how much work it would mean for both of them.

"For now Alan, I will show you one of the operational kits we have set up here as a demonstration of what will happen. You need to know everything, and once you know, you can then decide if you wish to continue, presuming that your visions keep coming."

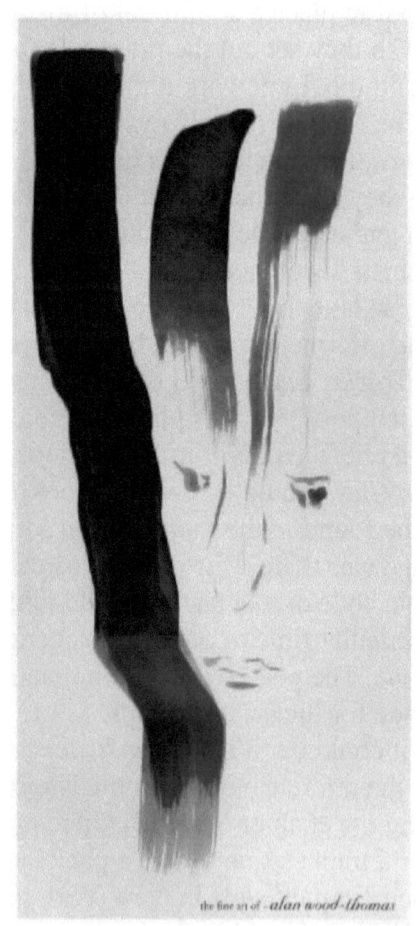

Nothingness haunts Being.

Jean-Paul Sartre

The Equipment

The Murder Luggage

Jacques then took Alan into a side room. Laid out in an adjoining room, which they accessed through an unlocked door, was a simple unassuming travel case. No one was present, but this had clearly been sent out for him to understand the process. "Here you see is an example of what we call 'the equipment'. A case like this is prepared for every mission undertaken by an operative." Jacques explained. "Every detail is organized in advance, and placed into a mission case such as this. Every case varies in accord with the task, but essentially the core setup never varies.

Before him sat a sturdy, waterproof piece of luggage, not dissimilar to what the modern musicians use to protect their musical equipment. Lockable, the size of a large suitcase, and made from aluminum. Alan goes up to inspect, and clearly, the case in front of him had been well used.

"Open it," said Jacques. Which he does.

Inside was lined with molded rubber. It had compartments for every specific thing an agent would need. "May I?" asked Alan. Jacques handed him some fine leather gloves to wear and indicated for him to inspect everything.

Alan took great care to extract and inspect every single compartment. The knife, razor sharp, and eleven-inch blade, with a metal handle. High grade, forged steel, it was a precision weapon. The coveralls, the ethanol, and the ether, along with towels used with both during an assassination. It all fitted into the lid, that also had binoculars, a fold-out seat, and a notebook. They all went into their appropriate compartment, and a leather strap made sure they stayed in place during transit.

In the base, all the ancillary items. A compass, road maps, a phrase book for the relevant country, cash, passports with a false name but with the photo still to be applied, obviously for the exit of the country by the agent. There was even canned food, a small burner, and even coffee with a tube of condensed milk. Everything was there for an agent to set up shop without the need to connect with anyone for any reason. It would seem the less contact with the locals, the better.

Jacques began to explain the process. "A local operative, someone who would not see or meet the agent, will set the case for that job into a prearranged location, sometimes buried, sometimes weighted and left in a river, or the sea. Always it is in a quiet spot away from curious eyes.

"When the job is done, the agent returns the case to the same spot, and leaves the country, using the false passport. He will place into it a photo to match his disguise. The official 'stamp' that goes over his photo is applied with the correct ink, which is also provided, and this makes a forgery that is more than sufficient for his hop to the next country. Here he collects another prepared passport, which is waiting for him in a security locker, for the next leg of his journey.

"We do not use women for the actual procedure," explained Jacques. "This is not because they are incapable, it is simply that the task will sometimes require significant physical strength. If a woman is pitted against a trained SS officer who wakes up, for example, she would need to use a gun. Our instructions are perfectly clear, only a knife is to be used, and the throat is to be cut."

He then took out some items and showed exactly how it worked. "Please note two bottles, Ether and Chloroform. There is no Chloroform present here, as we create this immediately prior to sending out a case. (chloroform has a ten-day life cycle before it degrades) It is a simple procedure, and it also means there are no pharmaceutical records of a person purchasing anesthetic. The ether is for two reasons, the first is for when the agent is in the field for more than a week, he will need to use the ether to stabilise the Chloroform. The second use is to wipe an area clean, and make sure there are no fingerprints left behind. Specifically, where the agent is staying must have nothing to connect him to the target.

The agent uses the chloroform/ether mix on the towel, which he places over the nose and mouth of the target as he slashes their throat. "This paralyzes the vocal chords, and while not instantaneous, it gives a degree of flexibility. For example, if there is a mistake, or perhaps the target has worn a protective brace, the chloroform makes the mark unable to react or call out.

If necessary, the individual is held down for the minute it takes for them to be rendered unconscious. Should they be able to resist the chloroform, the point of the knife can be used to cut the carotid artery, which will also render the target immobile. This is also a failsafe if we find a client out of bed. If you grab a person with chloroform over their face and place a knife at their throat, and tell them not to struggle, or else, it is amazing how many will not struggle. Truly, it is an extraordinary thing."

Alan knew that Jacques was speaking from long experience. He said nothing but simply listened as the Maquis leader continued.

"Regardless, the agent must have the person placed into their bed and will cut the throat at that point. And why is this? The clearest signal must be sent out to those who know the man that if you are a Nazi or a collaborator, then you cannot sleep soundly. No other weapon is to be used, the friends of the deceased must know and recognize it is the Maquis at work. We may not find them all, but they will live in the fear that we might." Then Jacques moved on to the other items in the case.

"Here we find the binoculars, kerosene stove, cans of food, etc. These allow the agent to camp without having to leave his position for many days. We must know the precise movements of the target, which in the case of many of them is straight forward. The Nazi is not a creative creature, and will very often follow a set pattern of behavior.

"Basic tools, for lock-picking, pliers for fence cutting, screwdrivers, a hammer with a screw driver in the handle, a small crowbar, screws, nails, etc. are all in this small portable toolkit. (He opens it to show the items) These are the necessary break-in tools, and there is even a basic multi-meter in here for the agent to test the phone wires for an alarm signal. There is even a collapsible backpack for carrying everything the agent will need from his room to the job.

"In getting themselves into position, the agent must not use public roads or public transport. Most agents move cross country on a motor bike, some prefer a bicycle. Other simply hike in and hike out. We place no determination on HOW a person gets into position, only that they must not be seen getting there.

"Of course, the equipment itself is entirely portable, and the agent must not leave a single thing behind. They will use the ether to rub down any surfaces in the hide. If they have had to rent a room to observe a target, they will do so under a false name, pay only with cash and preferably wear gloves at all times. Finger prints and hair are the only likely connection between an agent and a target, but if none are left at the scene, or in the room where they stay, connecting the job to someone staying in a room is impossible. All agents take great care to leave everything clean and free of evidence.

"When an agent has decided everything is in place, they proceed with the job. But if at any time any significant criteria is broken, they must abort, and a new agent will be sent in at a later date. Such things as a relative arriving, the target changing their routine significantly, anything that makes the end goal uncertain means we reset and restart.

"If it is a particularly difficult spot to get to, an agent may well go into the mountains or the country and camp out for a few weeks, returning later to see if the mark is more accessible. We leave the actual timing of the execution up to them. The criteria, it must be at night, they must be executed in their beds, and no one can see you coming or going during the process.

"Obviously, when the agent is ready to commit, he arrives at the scene, puts on the coveralls, hair net, and mask. In particular, the covering over the shoes has a sheepskin sole, which ensures no shoe size or shoe pattern can be isolated. There must be nothing that allows for hair or anything identifiable to the agent be left behind. When the police come and see it is clearly an assassination, they will then look for forensics in and about the house. They will look for foot prints, hair residue, and fingerprints. When they find none, they will scratch their heads, and place it in the file with all the other murders that have the same pattern."

Alan asked the obvious. "Surely, after a few of these start to add up, someone up the chain will see a clear pattern, and more attention will begin to be paid to these assassinations?"

"Obviously," replied Jacques. "Do you know just how many murders are being committed in France and neighboring countries? There are dozens of small clandestine groups wanting revenge. There are many hundreds every month. As a result, we have certain knowledge that De Gaulle is soon to pass a bill of a general amnesty for all the Vichy supporters, and it contains severe punishment for vigilantes who break this.

"So how do we avoid the law? There are several well-placed members of our group high up in both Government and the Police. We do not act alone, Alan. However, should any agent be caught, even if they are willing to answer questions they do not know anyone further up the chain than their immediate superior. That is myself, and no one knows my name. They do not know who set the case out, who made the chloroform, or who issued the order. They know nothing but the mission.

"Unfortunately, if caught, we can do nothing to help them. However, the men know their families will be looked after. There have been a few odd incidents, despite all our precautions. What we do in this instance is to provide evidence of guilt to any detective who happens to be looking very closely at what has occurred. What is more, it is delivered to him at his office, placed on his desk in an unmarked file for his eyes only.

"This is normal procedure. When he sees the evidence of what the assassinated man has done, but more than this, when he realizes that this came from within his own station, he gets the general message that the matter has been taken care of.

"Organisation, Alan. It is everything. I show you this because you are trusted, and also because you need to know that should your visions continue, as we all hope they will, that everything down the line is taken care of. Nothing will ever come back on you or your family. No Nazi will ever get a sniff of what is happening and cause you personal problems. The only connection you will ever see in this entire organization will be myself, and even then, our meetings will be rare."

"I understand perfectly," said Alan. "What you are telling me is that by providing you with information, I am as much an assassin as the man who commits the act."

"Bien." Jacques agrees. "It is time to get you back home to your family, n'est ce pas?"

Genius is what a man invents when he is looking for a way out.

Jean-Paul Sartre

Assassination

The End of Two Collaborators

Number Three went to collect his case, marked with a simple red ball floating in the Rhone. He was within a few miles of his mark and had already arranged accommodation in a small bed and breakfast that overlooked the house. Ten feet to the other side of the ball, he took a boating hook and dragged up the equipment.

He didn't need to open it, but he removed the waterproof lining and sent it back down with the weight. He would need it again when he was finished. It now looked like ordinary travel luggage that he had strapped to his motor cycle as made his way to his apartment.

Once inside, he went through the itinerary, the mark, and confirmed the address. A little different, two clients needed servicing. Sitting in the darkened room, he opened the curtains enough for him to look out and begin his observation. He opened his envelope, one target, clearly drawn, the house, clearly drawn. Yes, there was no mistake. A short summary of the man's offenses gave the agent more than enough motivation to finish the work. The second one came with a copy of his Nazi record, which always included a photo. A more current one had been added, no question it was the same man. What an evil bastard, killing of people simply because they were competition. Yes, he absolutely deserved to breathe his last. Once the targets and both of their addresses were confirmed, he burned the drawings, files, and details then prepared himself for the wait.

What times did they leave their house and return? Who else lived there? What was the security? Did they have a dog? Every question had to be answered. As an agent, he needed to know before he walked into any job exactly where the mark was when he slept, who else would be there, and what might be around that could affect a clean outcome. Nothing must be left to chance.

The rules were simple: The throat must be slit as the man slept in his own bed. No one else was to be harmed or involved. All information must be obtained covertly, preferably with the agent in disguise, and no direct approach must be made towards the Mark, or anyone close to him. It was a game of patience, waiting for and creating the right opportunity.

It was the oddest thing, but almost none of the war criminals had a wife or girlfriend who slept with them. They were all loners, to a man. Possibly it was their utter and complete lack of intimacy, or possibly it was simply after all the cruelty they had inflicted, a part of them expected that another would take the chance while they were vulnerable. In the case of the good brothers visiting them with justice, this was indeed the truth.

Number Three was unsure of why Number Two wanted to meet, perhaps to introduce this Number One? He really had no idea. It was a very unusual arrangement, but he assumed the former leader of the Maquis knew what he was doing. Might have been a new guy he was showing the ropes to. However, he had followed regulations to the letter. No one had seen him, and he made sure to take his cross country motorcycle through the back passes and trails to the collection point for the Case. Nothing else was different other than the appointed meeting.

Two in the one night was tricky, but the extra research gave the mill owners address and movements, and the first target had a nice set routine that was very easy to work with. Not even a lock on the window! The man had no fear of being found out. It seemed like the swine who caused the death of all those children didn't even have trouble sleeping at night. It took only three days of observation to be certain of a clean kill.

The mill owner was a drunk, in a locked house. He slept alone at the back and had a dog, but the barbiturates from the kit that he had cut into the meat would settle the animal down in short order. The two houses were not far apart, and the dog was already on its way to dream world. It would not pose a problem.

The first house was quite simple. A ladder had been needed to get to the balcony where the target's door lay wide open, and he had earlier noted there was one lying by the side of the house. It was virtually an invitation. He prepped his coveralls, pulled the slip-ons over the shoes, the hair net and mask over the head, and finally, he prepared the chloroform and towel, placing the soaked rag into a sealed container. And of course, the knife. Standard Bowie knife, eleven-inch blade, with an incised metal handle that would not slip.

Two o'clock in the morning, and like a cat, up he goes, onto the landing. In the darkened room the former policeman lay snoring, flat on his back. Perfect. Taking out the towel, holding the soaked area for the mouth and nose in one hand, and using the knife to keep up the other side, Number Three moved forward. In a single movement, the left-hand smothers the face, the target's eyes open wide in panic, and they automatically take a deep breath of shock.

His vocal chords are paralyzed. He cannot cry out or struggle back to consciousness fast enough to resist, but he knows. He knows this is payment. Number Three sees it in his eyes, the panic, the fear. The blade slips over the neck, cutting through the windpipe, and both carotid arteries. The eyes fade while the blood pours out over the towel. It cannot staunch the flow, of course, it is used to carry the chloroform, and to stop the blood spraying all over the assassin.

The task is done. He takes out the sea water, washes over his gloves to remove the worst of the blood, and rinses the knife. He then ritually blesses the man. Why? His crimes are paid for here on Earth, and it is up to the heavens to decide his fate in the afterlife.

After performing this death ritual so many times through World War Two, Number Three never really gave it much thought. He was a butcher in his outside life, and he even blessed the cattle he slaughtered. His real job, his real service to France, was ridding her of the corrupt and decadent creatures that were once the Nazi and its collaborators. Such evil must be removed, and like a surgeon cutting out cancer, he did this to help all of France heal.

For now, it was onto the next one, and sure enough, the dog had taken the meat and was fast asleep. This man had locks on his balcony door, but old barrel locks posed no problem, as he had master keys for those. This one slept lightly, so he had to move very gently into position. Even so, this particular mark awoke and managed a moment of struggle before the chloroform froze his voice, and the blade ended his life. Imagine, not only being responsible for the death of the Jewish owners from that last house but then putting in there the bastard that killed their children. Good riddance to this one.

Viva La France, Number Three muttered under his breath.

Out, moving as noiselessly as he came in, he takes all the coveralls off and places them into the carry bag. Tools go into their own bag, the knife is wiped clean. Towels go into the same bag as the bloody coveralls. They would burn with a little ether added. The only real point of risk was collecting the case, burning the wearables, and taking his case back to the drop-off point. This job went well, and he soon stopped to dig a small hole, start a fire, and eliminate any evidence.

Number Three did not suppose there was any forgiveness for those souls he had just sent to hell, but who knew? Maybe they had confessed, maybe they had remorse, and some part of the black hearts would find salvation. Even so, he said a small ritual prayer of cleansing over the burning coveralls, just in case.

The absolute truth? He really didn't care anymore. This work is what gave his life purpose and meaning, and the act of execution was a cleansing of his own sins, his own failings. As he was told so many years ago, when Number Two recruited him, "The day you start to enjoy this, revel in the blood, this is the day you must stop. You are in the service of France, removing her enemies. It is a job, not a joy."

When the war had ended, and he was still called to perform his usual duties on the collaborators, he did ask Jacques if they should now allow the authorities to look after these matters. He never forgot the words, "And then what? They will do nothing. And what are the consequence of this inaction? These creatures will raise black hearted children, their evil will seep from them like a poison, and ruin the innocence in all around them.

"We do not do this as judges of the men who are guilty, their death is not our purpose. We are stopping their evil effect on our culture, our people, and our children. We remain in the service of France, and though the tide has turned, there is still the debris littering our shores that make our world ugly and misshapen. We are simply the ones who clean up the mess."

It made sense. Number Three was perfectly happy to continue his work and remained confident in Number Two doing the leg work to ensure no innocents were harmed. The equipment case is once more wrapped in waterproof, a weight is tied to it, and it is thrown into the same spot as where he collected it just five days earlier.

On his motor cycle, with the morning light showing over the horizon, he made his way out of the woods and back to his shop in Paris. Another job well done.

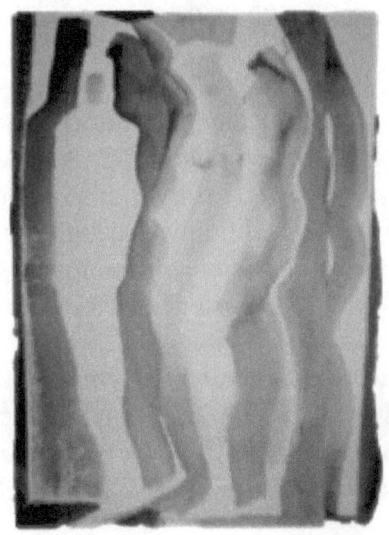

Every human endeavor,
however singular it seems,
involves the whole human race.

Jean-Paul Sartre

New York - 1948

Aftermath of Lyon

The old man looked up over a cup of coffee his son had made and started painting the picture in words of what life had been like back then, just before Cyrus had been born. "I was surprised to find commissions coming through from Carlebach's and it was here that I met Katzenbach. He seemed keenly interested in many things, but what surprised me is that he appeared to know about the 603d. This was highly classified, so I presume he dropped hints merely to let me know that he knew. This happened immediately prior to the family moving out to Connecticut, and indeed the finance from this is what allowed it.

"Now, of course, I understand Nicholas (Katzenbach) was in a position of great influence and apart from his own deep compassion for the plight of the Jews post war, I suspect there was a political advantage to be gained for him in some way. Certainly, he had a backdrop of money and influence that you could feel, even though he was not personally wealthy. He went out of his way to befriend my family, and brought many clients to visit, particularly when we moved up to Connecticut.

"My writer friends, Kerouac, Burroughs, Harrington, they were all finding greater success, but to be honest, while I enjoyed their company, my heart was in the visions. This became the thing that really made my life complete. Yes, I was grateful for the money the art provided, and I loved the work, even teaching the talentless women because as you know, it had certain benefits."

Cyrus wanted to jump in and ask the details about the affairs, of which he understood there were many. It always made him curious how his mother could be so devoted to a man who had not even the slightest sense that monogamy was important, or even desirable. However, his father kept on talking. "Yet the whole time, my deepest attention was caught up in what would come next. And the tension, *what if this time it went wrong?* I was part of an entire world so divorced from the existence of the common man that I may as well have been living on another planet.

"You cannot understand how this makes you FEEL. On one level, powerful, on another, vulnerable. I want you to understand, Little Cy, you are the only one to whom I ever spoke of these things. I was sworn to tell no-one, but we need to connect with one Soul here on Earth, or else we will float away in our dreams."

Cyrus finally had the real question he wanted to know an answer to. "What I cannot find to be true is that you are living a life based on a spiritual experience, you are living for these visions, and yet you refuse to accept the possibility of a God or a divine agent? I simply cannot see how this can be. The two things just do not add up."

"You want me to recite the Agnostics prayer? Please God, if there is a God, save my Soul, if I have a Soul?" Alan laughs at the child before him. How can anyone grasp how evil the Nazi were unless you saw it first hand. "My visions came from a place deep within me. From God? Maybe it was from Satan? Have you even considered Satan was doing this because he wanted his children to come back home to him in Hell?"

They laugh. Nietzsche and the abstracts of *'God is dead'* was a powerful dialogue for Alan. "There was a quote Jacques used to remind me of on a regular basis, *'He who fights with monsters might take care lest he thereby become a monster. And if you gaze too long into an abyss, the abyss gazes back into you.'* This is why everything was checked, and silence between all parties involved was something considered to be of a paramount importance.

"This is the essence, that by reminding ourselves again and again of what we do, and why we do it, we stop ourselves from falling into the abyss. Jacques used to make sure he came here at least once a year to review the project, go over the details, and he also showed me where a particular assassin worked or lived. He wanted me to go, in disguise, to see WHO was completing the visions I saw. Why did he do this? It reminded me again and again that this was no casual matter.

"There are real people, putting their lives at risk for an ideal. We were not just killing the Nazi, we were killing their fascist dream. Their death is a signal sent out to those who knew them *'You will get your throat cut while you sleep'*. This was a MESSAGE we were sending to all of them. It was a reminder to THEM. It was a message to THEM, the ones we did not find, the ones who were not thrown up for sacrifice.

"Jacques kept me in the loop to keep MY feet on the ground. He nurtured me, and I know commissions came my way because of the work I did for the resistance. I know there was a hidden network of people, whose names I will never know, whose faces I would never recognize, all quietly working to end this insane ideal that the Nazi espoused, which was simply: *Might makes Right.*"

Alan paused, and wondered if the message was finally getting through. "Look about you, my son. Do you see a world where force of arms is no longer the controlling lever for nations? Force of trade is the new power, and despite how much contempt we may have for governments, how do you think someone would go now-a-days going out and saying *'Homosexuals, Jews, Blacks and Slavs need to be exterminated'*?"

"It was not GOD who created this change, it was thousands and thousands of dedicated individuals who stood up and said that the ideals of the Nazi were WRONG. 'We' are *'of the people, for the people, by the people'*, not our government. 'We' are the ones responsible for the decisions, not the education system, not the propaganda. If each individual German had stood up and said way back in 1938 after Crystal Night, *'This is wrong!'* Hitler would never have reached the level of insanity he unleashed.

"It is 'we' who decide the future Little Cy. And 'we' decide this with our ACTIONS." Alan had leaned forward from his bed to drive the point home, but even this tired him. He lapsed back into the pillows, and sought refuge in the past. "I think you know the general framework regarding my return to New York after the trip to Lyon."

> *In life man commits himself and draws his own portrait, outside of which there is nothing. No doubt this thought may seem harsh to someone who has not made a success of his life. But on the other hand, it helps people to understand that reality alone counts, and that dreams, expectations and hopes only serve to define a man as a broken dream, aborted hopes, and futile expectations.*
>
> Jean-Paul Sartre

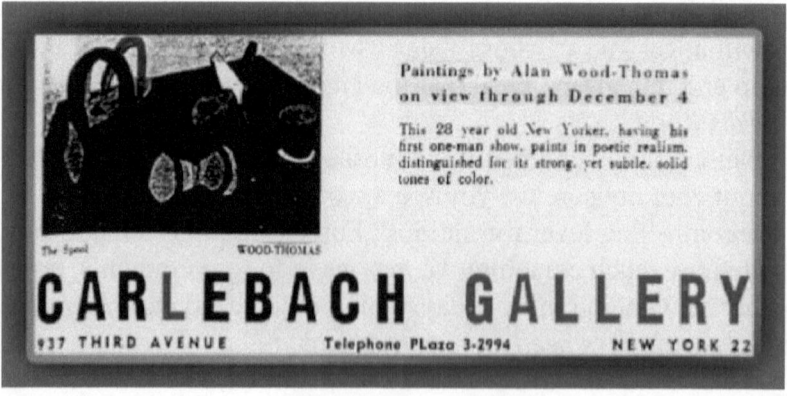

The Return to New York

Notes from Cyrus:

*F*ew were more surprised by the outcome of this journey to Paris and Lyon than Alan had been. To be honest, even before he left he suspected his visions were connected to the Maquis. The men he saw had that cold, emotionless aspect you saw in Nazis and collaborators. When you choose to murder innocent people, and in particular children, it marks your Soul with a callousness. Just as you cannot hide a natural smile, you cannot hide natural cruelty.

Alan arrived back home to a demand for more work, and he did not have a lot of time to consider things. He presumed that the visions were probably done with, the connection with the Maquis finally over, and it was back to a normal existence for himself and his family.

But the experiences kept coming, sometimes two a month, but on average, once every month without fail. And every time, the vision married up to a Nazi or a collaborator who had slipped the net. His drawings made the target perfectly clear to all, and as the Germans kept such rigorous documentation, it was very easy to marry a photo to a sketch and be certain that they had the right man. His ability to draw in such precise detail meant there would be no mistakes, and these men who had apparently vanished could now be discovered by comparing his sketch to the photo in their war record.

Jacques did open a small investigation business, near to Fifth Avenue, in a nondescript building. There was no sign, other than a small brass plaque, similar to what you find on a doctors reception rooms. From what Alan was given to understand, in the immediate post-war period, finding lost property was in hot demand, but he never went in to see. No direct connection could be made between himself and Jacques in New York, or anywhere.

The simple system of coded messages worked exceedingly well, and Alan suspected that the secretary who did all the running around was herself a former agent. But he never spoke with her or had any formal meeting at or near the offices.

On the odd occasions, perhaps every eighteen months or so, a meeting would be scheduled. Jacques would be in New York on investigation business and a coded message would be sent. Alan would catch a country train, and meet up, or if it were more sensitive he would go to Le Guardia and hop on a private plane owned by one of Jacques wealthy clients. On board might be Jacques, or Alan might be flown to a location where they *could meet. Sometimes the meeting might go for an hour, but usually, it was a relaxed affair over lunch, and it went for half a day.*

During these sojourns, Jacques would detail any changes to the organization, specifically focussing on any new members, and Alan's opinion was asked about any number of things. It would seem that Jacques wanted him to vet every agent, believing that Alan's ability to see things extended not to just visions. No agent was ever someone who had not been known to the existing members for at least a decade, and over time some of the originals needed to be replaced.

Perhaps it was illness or a new marriage where unexplained absences would not be acceptable, or the individual passed away, but new agents were needed on a regular basis. If Alan looked at a photo and was unsure, occasionally Jacques would arrange for the fellow to be in the US, and, in disguise, Alan would meet him and size him up personally. For whatever the reason, if Alan did not approve of the agent, he was not used.

There was one exception, and this led to the shutting down of the whole operation.

For the present time, in those immediate post-war years, upon his return Alan found many new doorways opening for him in New York.

We take up the story again some days later where Little Cy was seeing his father in Connecticut, during his last months:

The Philosophy of the Resistance

The Raison D'Etre of the Work: as Seen By Jacques

Alan Wood-Thomas looked out at the bright morning. He smiled, a deep love for the simple things ruled his heart, and it touched everything he did. It was yet another paradox for his son. This man, so refined, so elegant, yet so ruthless. Cyrus has to ask, "I just find it so hard to marry up what I see before me, you as the refined artist versus you as the cold hearted killer. You knew what would happen when you passed on the information. You were happy for the result, and remained at peace and untroubled. But honestly, do you still have no concerns about your actions, given you are so close to moving on?"

His father laughs. Once more, the youth know nothing, even though they believe they know everything. But he was like that once, so long ago. "I had the same question mark when I was a teenager, and I first met Jacques. I knew what he did, even at age sixteen. (Alan waves his hand, like a magician clearing obstacles from his vision) He was stationed in France after leaving Spain, just prior to the war getting underway. He told me then that there are things in this world that must be met, and dealt with. But it was not until Crystal Night that we all fully grasped what true evil was in the Nazi heart.

"Would you question me killing a deadly snake about to bite you? I don't think so. The problem today is that people have already forgotten what a snake the Nazis were. Do you remember the footage of the Berlin Olympics in 1936? I am sure you do. Jacques was over there, doing what he does. The Maquis stood with Churchill from the earliest of times, because we all knew what Hitler was doing.

"But most people, including the Olympic Federation, only saw the grandeur, the success! They saw how Hitler had pulled Germany from the depression and was able to spend a fortune on staging the first spectacular Olympic Games, the one that was to become the model for the future. It was a phenomenal success for propaganda, and many left thinking THIS is what the world needed to shake itself out of the financial misery. So a blind eye was turned to the labor camps, the treatment of Jews and social minorities.

"Jacques was there with my father in 1938 when the pogroms started, and it firmed up his resolve. There was a snake in the house of Europe, and if unchecked it would poison everyone. Field Marshall Von Blomberg, the Nazi War Minister who had to quit his post because his wife was found making pornographic photos, had already talked openly about Germany taking back what was rightfully theirs. He talked openly about making France a war zone.

"He was also the one that kept the Nazi divisions out of the Spanish Civil War, and so only a few planes were sent, along with advisors to assist Franco. Von Blomberg openly stated they needed to focus on building up their home forces. Already he had eyes on France. Already he was arming the snake, getting it ready to strike. Those fools who argue that Hitler was just an opportunist ignore the obvious, he was creating an army, and not for the purpose of defending his borders.

"But Goring and Himmler wanted Von Blomberg gone, and so they let him marry the former prostitute and then showed him the photos of her posing naked for a Jew. He left the halls of power and eventually realized he was just a Nazi pawn, but then he met Prutzmann, the evil snake who in 1944 was to be put in charge of the Nazi Werewolves. He infected this man with the notion of making France the place to destroy any resistance to the Nazi ideals. France was the evil that must suffer. As a result, Prutzmann, and others like him, just wanted to see France burn.

"This is when Jacques first formulated the underlying plan for the resistance, even back then. The Maquis in Spain never attacked openly. They knew the power of a small force was distraction, weakening the resolve of the enemy, creating small chinks in the armor that caused the leadership to have trouble from the inside. And in truth, they used camouflage as a weapon of war well before the British or Americans.

"When I finally got to rejoin him in France during the war, he was instrumental in getting our inflatable decoys into position. More than this, he made sure the locals kept quiet, and that the Germans were continually fed with the wrong information. And what does this have to do with your question? Everything.

"I was his eyes and ears in the Allies. He was my eyes and ears in the resistance. Together we formed a powerful force, one that saved untold thousands of lives by helping bring that war to an early close. As much as I fought for America, I fought for France. The goal was to defeat the enemy, to cut the head off the snake. I was a child of the resistance, Little Cy, a child of war. I am still a child formed out of the stuff of death, whose mission never changed. I was born to kill the Nazi and any who sided with them.

"So for me, the death of a Nazi or a sympathizer was, and IS, as beautiful a thing as the rising sun over the fields. So there is no contradiction in my head or heart. To keep the weeds from the garden, those weeds must die.

Little Cy just sighs. He knows this, his father knows he knows, but the contradiction is still there. Just as his father still refused to believe in a God, even though he was regularly taken out of his body and demonstrated miracles of remote viewing. He chose to see things in a way his son could never fully accept, but what else could he do?

It would not be until 2005, many years later, that Little Cy would see the film 'Munich' and realize that the casual words dropped by his father at the time of that event were so significant. *"If we had been allowed in, it would have been so different. No-one but the terrorists would have died."* Back then Cyrus was not sure if he was talking about the army days, or Jacques. Alan had dropped snippets all along, like when his son was staying in France, Cyrus had been asked to 'drop a note' into a library.

He knew what that note was for, and felt utterly helpless. He was not a good field operative at all, even with such a small task. But that episode came back to him as he watched 'Munich' for the first time. He knew the note going to the library had been a message from his father, just as the comment by Alan during the Munich massacre was also a simple message.

But after this film came out, something clicked inside the son. Cyrus Wood-Thomas just KNEW the story had to be told. He was the only person in the family to know the details, as his Father had told no one else. Yes, his mother knew Alan regularly had the visions and sent the information somewhere, but Cyrus was the sole person to know what it was for.

And paradoxically, when Alan was alive, this is what always led into the arguments over God, salvation and the spiritual truths that flowed through each person's lives. Little Cy firmly advocating a force for good, his father calmly refuting, believing men made the decisions and bore the responsibility. His view was simple: Good and evil would always coexist, but the decisions men made determined how well the good survived. To this end, the survival of what WAS good is what mattered.

Camouflage

The Art of Deception

Alan rested for a few days. Cyrus had to earn money and was out painting houses to bring in a few coins and help the family. When he came home, doing the hard work he was not conditioned for, he was tired, so ate, then slept, and was up early the next morning. When the weekend came round, his father was happy to see his boy and continue with another round of dialogue

This is how it used to be, the family worked together so that the family survived. In the present world, the dog eats dog *'me first'* mentality has taken over so much of people's lives. Children no longer keep parents at home when they are old, they no longer meet every weekend for dinner to talk with relatives and friends. We have become isolated in the very freedoms our forbearers won through their sacrifice and courage.

"Did I ever tell you WHY I wanted so much to be in the 603d?" Alan asked as they sat outside drinking coffee. It was a gray day, and cold, so he was well wrapped. To be honest, it was not a question Cyrus had ever really considered, but given that his father badly burned his foot in order to not ship out with the mechanics, as he thought about this, there must have been a powerful reason.

"Before I left France, before the war started, I had a general talk with Jacques about how to wage the battle in Spain. He opposed open conflagration and devoted himself to what we would now call terrorist tactics. But he had a very different agenda to most.

"His notion on how to win a war came from his study of Judo. The trick is to turn your opponents own strength against himself. The Nazi were in Spain, controlling the intelligence gathering for Franco. Jacques got the notion of deception, and after all, camouflage IS a French word. It is fitting for a Frenchman to work with it.

"He would arrange for casual conversations and odd items to fall in the path of people he knew were collaborators. This dropping of clues and hints he knew would reach further up the chain, and someone high in intelligence would think they were very clever putting together the jigsaw that Jacques had intentionally fed him. The thing is, where the supposed insurgents would be gathered to strike would be where some division of Franco's army was marching.

"On more than a few occasions, the Germans gave orders for Franco's guns to bombard Franco's own soldiers. Or German bombers would blast a village that was completely empty, while the real attack happened many miles from there. His favorite trick was to convince a German intelligence operator that one of their own collaborators was a spy for the resistance so that the man was tortured for information he didn't have before he died.

"I saw first hand how effective his tactics were, and when I got wind that the 603d was being formed and that it needed artists, well, this was the place for me."

Alan laughed, remembering a time immediately prior to the Battle of the Bulge, where the 603d pulled off one of the greatest deceptions of the war."I always remember my old friend, Fred Fox, dressing up as a General from the 6th Armored Battalion. We needed to create the illusion that this division was building up in the area, so he and a driver go into the hotel of a known collaborator, and basically steal his wine, and make a huge commotion in order to anger the man. His Jeep has the codes for the 6th Armor, his clothes were that of a General from that Battalion, it surely looked as it there were there.

"Of course, the first thing the collaborator does is to report a General in the area to his superiors, and German Intelligence has to radically revise where they believe the 6th Armored is. They 'thought' it was in Brittany (where it was) but now they place it square on the map, right where there is in truth a seventy mile 'hole' in the defensive line. They could have walked through singing songs of the Fatherland, but they didn't.

"Instead, they pulled the 48th and 19th Divisions and part of the 36th away from Metz, the real target. For ten days, and for far longer than we thought possible, the 603d played the role of the 6th Battalion. No subterfuge had ever worked so long, but between the 12th and 22nd of September in 1944, we held out the illusion of a vast army.

"Then, the unthinkable. The Germans blew up their OWN bridge at Remich, and retreated behind Moselle. This meant they could no longer advance their armor, which meant Patton's vulnerable flank was safe. The opening into Germany for the Allies was through Moselle.

"The 603d, without weapons, with only rubber tanks and sound effects, had pushed the mighty German army out of Luxembourg!" Alan laughed, so obviously proud of his work in France. "This is the Art of Deception, and it saved untold lives, on both sides of the conflict."

Annabelle had brought in supper, and Alan continued with a few stories of wartime France. She was having to spoon feed him now, his muscles had deteriorated so badly. His head even needed to be propped up in case he suffocated. Yet he somehow put up with the interminable condition.

Cyrus could see in his mother's eyes the obvious love and affection she had for her man, and he knew that for her, he was her hero. Well it was true, his father WAS a hero, unsung, unnoticed for the most part, but every fibre of the mans being stood out as someone you just had to admire.

RESTITUTION

The Story of Jacques

> ***Jewish Political Studies Review 19:1-2 (Spring 2007)***
> *Less than 20 percent of the value of Jewish assets stolen by the Nazis and their collaborators has been restored. At least $115-$175 billion (2005 prices) remains unreturned despite numerous clear and explicit international agreements and country promises made during World War II and immediately thereafter. Even the highly publicized resurgence of restitution efforts since the mid-1990s resulted in the return of only 3 percent of Holocaust property. A key reason for these meager results during both periods was the failure to make a unique, comprehensive, and timely effort to deal adequately with an event unequaled in the annals of modern history-the extermination of more than two-thirds of continental European Jewry and the confiscation of nearly all of its assets.*

Alan was nearing the end of his time. Cyrus had been staying for many months, doing the odd jobs such as house painting, but finally, the old man was coming to the final stages of ALS. On this day, he chose to talk about a very different thing: He spoke directly about Jacques and his role in the operation.

"Now, you know I have never given you his true name, nor have I really said much about the man personally. I feel you need to know more because this is the real story behind this whole situation. The only reason we were so successful for so long was because of this man. He was extremely well-regarded in the French Government and in many of the European nations.

"Jacques was a big man, very powerful. Even in his old age, only a fool would try to jump him. And he was still quick. He walked like a cat on the prowl and saw every little detail. He knew many in the artistic community, and was a sort of Renascence Man because his associations and abilities crossed many layers of society. Core to his simple belief was that, while the Nazi and collaborators must pay, those who suffered under their hands must be reconciled in some way. This meant not only returning assets where possible, but also letting the family members who survived KNOW that the debt had been repaid in the only way possible, with death.

"The greater part of his external work was restoring stolen property, and he worked in the French Government specifically in this area. He prepared the legal cases for people, pro bono, and if they got property back, some would contribute towards the cause. It was never demanded, but it was enough to finance the entire operation.

"Sadly, and obviously, I could not take any cash from our collaboration to help my family. My work was purely voluntary, however, I received commissions and sold work to people that were pointed my way by unseen hands. I presumed some sales came via Jacques encouragement behind the scenes. We always had enough to get by, and I have no regrets because it is morally wrong to profit in any way by the loss of another. I would be no better than the Nazi if I did.

"People think of the Nazi machine as an evil empire, but at its heart, it was driven by greed. Money, power, property, art, jewels triggered the avarice, and over all, vanity ran the show: These are the things that drove each individual in that organization, not some idealism for a perfect world. That was the excuse they gave each other. The ideals were a smokescreen that allowed the individuals to hide behind the reality of their lust.

"Their lust drove them to rape and plunder with no regard for those they hurt or destroyed. Was it fair, could anyone imagine it was fair, right or just for the war to end and these creatures to just walk away? What about the damage they did to so many millions of innocents?

"You are the only one, Little Cy, the only one I have trusted with this. One day you will understand, probably the day you are not stuffed to the gills with ideals.' Alan laughed. "But know this, we all have our role to play in the great circus. I was not 'driven' to do this work, for me it seemed perfectly natural. And the greater reason for this was not the people that died, but because of the people who LIVED.

"Jacques understood the REAL work was redress. So many families had property returned, lives restored, missing pieces of the puzzle filled in. We did far more than remove the evil creatures, my boy, we were part of a process that restored people to their dignity. You cannot believe how DEGRADING it is for a child to know their parents were systematically murdered, raped, pillaged, and treated like garbage. And then they are told to beg like dogs for scraps of justice to be handed to them after the war.

"Did you know that in the 1950's the official repatriation commission, which was set up after World War ONE, was full of Nazis? Can you imagine that? Can you IMAGINE how a person feels asking for their property back from one of the damn creatures that stole it from them in the first place, and then having to PROVE you are worthy to receive it? As a result of our work, people started paying attention to proper restitution, proper repatriation for the families of the poor souls who lost everything.

"Why was it not just done? Why did so many European countries make it so difficult for justice to be gained by the relatives of those humiliated and broken by the Nazis? Well, because there were still a lot of these creatures lurking in the corridors of the very courts and offices making the repatriation decisions.

"We were sending THEM a message. So in the end, my true vision was a kindness. Cruel to be kind. Ending the lives of some 300 Nazi was part and parcel of clearing the decks for greater justice. For one, it meant those in power knew they were not safe sitting on a pedestal. If they had a skeleton in the closet, they had better beware. We did not just administer justice, little Cy, we CREATED it."

The great man paused. He would become weak from simply talking now, and he needed regular bouts of sleep to keep going. His eyes closed, and he slipped away into dreams. Cyrus just sat there, contemplating. He felt the love from his Father, yet still had trouble reconciling this with the actions the man took in his life. Even when what he was saying made sense.

You cannot harbor a snake in your house and expect happiness. If it was true, that some Nazis were still in the corridors of power, then he could see that the fear of being discovered, of waking in fright one evening to find a man with an eleven inch bowie knife about to descend on your throat, maybe this DID have a role in creating a better society.

Alan stirred briefly, and added, "Annabelle knew I had visions and did something with them, but she never asked specifically. She is not stupid, she had a fair idea, but she never said anything, and not once did I hear her complain. I cannot tell her the full story, it would break her heart, but in truth she knows. She knew what I was when we were married."

The Miami Job

The Beginning of the End

Alan was really coming to the end of his time. It was difficult watching the last stages of ALS at work, the tremors, the loss of control. But inwardly the man fought on. Cyrus had been given a clear insight into his thinking, but he still knew very few details of what actually happened. Finally, perhaps because he knew the end was close, his father seemed willing to talk in detail about actual events.

Cyrus knew that in the entire twenty-five or so years the operations had been underway, there had not been one single failure. Not one man had ever been caught, not one nominated fugitive had escaped justice. There had been many close calls, some mistakes, a couple of times and operation had to be delayed of the agent swapped out. But then, right up to the closing stages of the operation, there had been such a total and complete failure in the chain of command. This was the Miami job.

Cyrus thought for a minute, then asked, "I remember that you gave a hint years ago of one of your visions not working out properly, because of protocols not being followed. I got the sense from you at the time that this was why the operation was shut down."

Alan looked up, "The Miami Job? No, this was not the reason. But it was around that time that the visions stopped. I have no idea why they started, and no idea why they stopped. Yet, at the same time that last and almost total disaster heralded the end of the operation. And I blame myself, Jacques had always said if I did not approve of an operative, he would not be used.

"Well, my gut told me not to use this man, but logic said he was the perfect solution for a difficult operation in South America. I gave my OK even though I had doubts. I still find it just extraordinary how this one man managed to overturn just about every single protocol he had sworn to uphold, and not even think twice about the sheer unmitigated stupidity of his actions.

"It had all started with the normal French assassin getting sick, and recommending a personal friend of his, an Italian he had known during the war. The man had done similar work in Italy. He was now living in the States, and Jacques had flown out from France to personally vet the man. He had his doubts, and asked me to go to the man's place of business, in disguise of course, and check the fellow out for myself.

"Like so many of our operatives, the man was self-employed," Alan took up the story. "He had worked in the Italian resistance, this had been verified, and the man checked out as reliable. He had no pressing debts, and seemed to be financially well off. Things like this are very important, because a hungry man, a man who needed money, they will take shortcuts. They will also steal from the target, or from someone else, which confuses the clear reason for the assassination. They create ripples and problems. And when an operation is meant to be a simple 'in and out affair', they hang about looking for some opportunity to make money.

"But while he checked out, something inside myself was unsure about this fellow. I know now what it was, the oldest sin, sloth. The man was incredibly lazy and simply agreed to our protocols without the slightest intention of ever following them. No alcohol, well, turns out he was an alcoholic. Only a knife to be used, in the man's bed, well, he completely missed that one, and shot the target as well as an innocent. No profit was to be made from the job, and the man went out of his way to pocket a barrel load of cash. What a mess.

"The target was a Nazi in South America, in a particularly difficult spot, well up the Amazon. The man had had a plantation, and it was suicide to go up there to complete the mission, but the fellow came into town once every month. The arrangement was made to finish the job in the man's hotel room.

"This was an SS Nazi, truly evil, and by what we understood, he was continuing to commit atrocities on the locals. They were too terrified to take the matter up with the police, but the local police would have been bought and paid for regardless. His own farm was a fortress, and getting there undetected would have been impossible. There was only one way in, up the river, and guilty paranoid people paid to know who was travelling.

"We considered something exotic, like a National Geographic expedition, but if someone checked and found anything suspect, they would be killed. This Hauptsturmführer was as ruthless as they came. In the end, we had a man go into the area posing as a copra buyer as a scout. He discovered the target came to town once a month for supplies and whores. What's more the man always stayed at the same hotel, in the same room, on the last three days of every month. A small variation from protocol, but we were finding the Nazi in South America were becoming far more vigilant, and more difficult to get to.

"It was not just ourselves. There were a few other organisations intent on tracking Nazis down and bringing them back for justice. Our 'justice' was well known by now, and so elaborate precautions were being taken by some of the targets. Never sleeping in the same room two nights in a row, having trained dogs, electrified fencing, locked bars on doors and windows, these were some of the issues to get around. Plus the local constabulary were effectively owned, and any slip-up would mean our agent would just vanish.

"In essence, it meant that we had done our job well. We put fear into their hearts. At the same time, it required a good deal more planning for each mission. It also meant that we had far greater expenses to meet, and even though Jacques always found the money, the zeal of those who had been wronged had abated, and there were very few unsettled properties or valuable items left to repatriate. So in this regard, the financial support for the operation was shutting down.

"Jacques carried almost no business through his New York offices now, and keeping the doors open was no longer an option. Men like Pierre Houpert had passed on, and any money they had bequeathed to the ongoing work had run out. It was under these conditions that we agreed to meet the Italians expenses, and gave him the standard instructions. The equipment would be delivered to a small office we had rented for the mission, next to the hotel.

"It was all standard procedure, and the Italian considered it a bit of a holiday. He went down but as bad luck would have it, the fellow got a flu and sent his mistress to town to do the buying. Can you believe the stupid Italian fancied his chances with her, and rather than abort the mission he spent three days wining and dining her, and THEN he kidnapped the poor woman, bringing her back with him to New York, sending the German a message that he owned her now. If he wanted her back, it would cost him.

"On one level, smart. The target was enraged and booked the earliest possible flight up to Miami, where he was told the woman was being held. He came with his bodyguard, of course, and was stupid enough to bring the money. Of course, the Nazi fully intended to kill the kidnapper, but he wanted the woman back first.

"We knew nothing of the changed arrangements, nothing of the kidnapping, and only found out how badly botched the whole thing was when it hit the newspapers. This was an absolute disaster. Every protocol had been breached. An innocent had been dragged in, both the woman and his body guard. He was nowhere near his bed, everything was just wrong.

"Turns out the Italian thought it would be an easy enough job, the guy comes in with money he can use, he kills him, sends the woman back or keeps her if she wants to stay. In his mind, a simple solution that serves him well. The reality was, the man arrives with his body guard, there is an almighty brawl in the private hotel room, and while he kills the German, he also kills the bodyguard. The fool used a gun without so much as a silencer, and they too had guns.

"He gets wounded, and there is blood and evidence all over the crime scene, and afterward the woman is found and taken into custody. She tells the police it was a kidnap plot, and it certainly looks that way, because that is exactly what it was. The Italian hotfoots it out of America, back to Italy with the cash, knowing he had completely stuffed it up.

"The equipment case was left in the office in South America, untouched. No signal was sent to the operative there to collect it, and the local Police found it and started asking questions. Of course, we did not have anything that tracked back to us, but even so, this absolute disaster showed us that the whole framework was starting to run down. It also sent out a huge red flag to those who had reason to fear us, a public slaying in a public place. Many of the rats started to bury themselves deeper in their holes.

"Plus, from our end, the ranks were thinning. We no longer had committed members of the Maquis still working with us. Most were too old or dead. We no longer had the financing to ensure smooth operations. It all signalled the end. Whether it was something inside me that had clicked off, or if indeed it was simply that the time had come, the show was coming to an end. There was but one last job, and after that the visions ceased."

Little Cy looked up, he had never heard his father speak in such graphic details before about any specific job, but this 'last job' was dangling in front of him like a carrot. "Did you want to tell me about this one?" he asks.

Life has no meaning a priori… It is up to you to give it a meaning, and value is nothing but the meaning that you choose.

Jean-Paul Sartre

The Final Nazi

The Curtain Draws to a Close

The following day was when Alan had recovered enough to take up the tale. After an early fog, the day had brightened. The mist and cloud of the morning had given way to a cheery, clear day, still cool, but full of bird song. Cyrus' father had given this last question of the night before some considerable thought. Clearly there was more to it than met the eye, and he seemed to want to give things time before responding. "I can tell you what I know, I guess. It doesn't matter if the truth comes out now. This was our greatest secret, the WAY we operated, and the reason WHY we were so successful. As I had mentioned, many of the Nazi that had escaped to South America were now extremely wary. It was getting harder to be able to complete a job and we were needing ever more elaborate plots.

"This last vision was one of the most curious. I fly high above, no idea where, but as I come in to the continent below me I see the triple peak of Mount Illimani, so I know we are in La Paz, Bolivia. South America had been the place of so many visions now, as most of the Nazi appeared to have gone there to escape justice.

"By this time, the experience of these flying journeys was normal, but every single one had its own unique properties. Not one was exactly the same in shape or format to the other. The only common thread was seeing a person who would later be identified as a Nazi. The difficulty was in isolating the target. South America houses were communal affairs, but usually, the one nasty pig would stand out. Then there were some other households with several possibilities, several suspicious looking characters. This was the case in La Paz, the City of Peace.

"The city is situated in the bowl of surrounding hills, and in the background overlooking everything is the very imposing triple peak. The city is high, yet subtropical. The Spanish settled it, on top of an old Incan village, and it was central to many trading routes in the area." Alan laughed. "I found out a lot more about the place AFTER this job was done. Regardless, the vision took me to an area North of the city centre, a very expensive suburb by the looks, with small acreage properties and large houses in compounds.

"The house I am brought to is large, a mansion, and surrounded by a high electrical fence with automatic gates. The person who owns it is very security conscious. There is a Land Rover at the back, ex-army issue by the look, and in the garage, I can see a Mercedes limousine, blue, in immaculate order. It is a Pullman, brand new in 1969.

"This car of itself told me the man was concerned about assassination, because these 'presidential' limousines had bullet proof everything, and cost a small fortune. Only people who lived in fear bought them.

"Out the back, behind the immediate compound, there is a stable for horses, with riding gear propped onto rails that are under cover. The gate is locked to this. To the other side of the house, there was an out-building, servants quarters I presumed, with a Volkswagen Beetle by the shape of it under a tarpaulin.

"I turn and see the house, white stucco, Tuscan styled terra cotta roof. A cross between traditional Spanish architecture, but with Italian style statues used as fountains in ponds. The gardens are low beds, beautifully maintained, and the lawn is lush. I was surprised at the foliage, trees done with topiary, flower beds, and behind the servants quarters, a vegetable garden with fruit trees.

"I see the gardener there, weeding. Then my attention is drawn into the house, an old chef is preparing lunch by the looks, his hands shaking. He is old, and I wonder if this is the target. He drops a plate, and it shatters. A beautiful woman comes in, very Spanish looking, not Indian. She shakes her head at the old man, and let off a tirade of what seems abuse, waving her hands, then getting down to clean up the mess. She is clearly displeased with him.

"Is she the target? It is hard to know these things, but I make mental notes of their faces, and am prepared to draw both. Then she takes the food he had been preparing from the kitchen, and I follow behind her." Alan laughs again, recalling the event as if it were yesterday. "You know, I sometimes thought of myself as a ghost. I could see everything, but heard no sound, no sound at all. I could see the lips moving, I knew they were talking, but I was as deaf to them as I was invisible.

"The woman takes the food, and for some reason I can see it very clearly. It is mushroom soup. Why am I seeing mushroom soup? I learned long ago not to really question what is presented, everything I see may serve a purpose. She takes it to a man in his late 60's. Bingo! He had the look. I know without thinking this is the target." Alan paused and explained the Cyrus what 'the look' was.

"These Nazi, they all have an arrogance in their face. They all have a sense of superiority, and the way they treat others is more like they are dealing with cattle. I suppose this was why it was so easy for them to follow orders and kill the Jews. This man had this inborn superiority in spades. The woman clearly lived in fear of him, which told me that he was cruel. This was when it got really strange, he insisted she sit and watch him have his soup, and when he was finished he ordered her to take off her clothes, and he sexed her. Not with passion, he just bent her over the bed and took her from behind, like a dog.

"Clearly she accepted this was part of the job, and when he was done, she collected her clothes and left. She did not even stay to dress, and he seemed to expect her to leave. He then laid down, and fell asleep. I go over to his desk, and see correspondence, on company letterhead. Carl Roemer, and there are photos from a mine, and letters that are left out, all relating to operational matters."

Alan took a drink of his coffee, and gazed out from his room. He was sitting up today, it was cold despite the sunshine outside, but he was well rugged up. "I was feeling like a voyeur, but I was pulled back to the body, and drew everything as I always did. His face, round cheeks, jowls, red blush (I presumed from alcohol) and these small blue eyes with sandy hair, closely cropped. He was of a large build, square shoulders, clearly someone who worked out, and fit for what looked like almost seventy years, but as I drew him I had a feeling of revulsion.

"This was something that was not normal. I just see things, and record them, then hand them over. This fellow made me feel weird."

Alan paused, and stressed, "He really gave me the creeps, so I drew a couple of sketches of him, from different angles. And this is when I first experienced the really strange part, I saw in my minds eye two distinct faces. The one in the vision seemed to be superimposed with another, very different face. I drew them both. After many years, I had learned not to question these odd variations, and just do it. It was difficult because I knew that second face, I knew it well.

"I drew up the woman, the house, the chef, the gardener. I made a note of the image of the mushroom soup, and the routine the fellow seemed to have. Some hours later, another vision came. The same house, I am standing in the middle of the night on a balcony gazing in. The man is there, working, pacing up and down. He is clearly tired, yet it strikes me, he is an insomniac. He can't sleep.

"It makes sense now. He sexes the woman as a way to shut down his mind, and sleep. The man is wary, I can feel it. It is almost like he knows I am watching him. This was a first, no one ever gave me that feeling before. Of course, I am just a point of view floating in space. He cannot see me, but he is looking. Perhaps it was a permanent paranoia, I can't say. But I felt that, for the very first time, the watcher was being watched.

"I record all the tiny details, including the fact that I felt he knew I was there, and send it off for processing. It normally takes a week to three weeks before a vision is verified, but this took longer. It took almost three months. And here it became something extraordinary. The 'second' face, the one I recognised, was definitely that of Marin Bormann. It was the reason I was so puzzled.

"The photo in the Nazi files was a perfect match for what I saw, but the second face had no such connection. It was not found anywhere in the German war records. I now understood why Jacques had requested a personal meeting with this one, it was a first time an event like this had occurred.

"In extraordinary circumstances, his personal friend in New York, a wealthy industrialist, a well known prominent Jew, would lend him his private jet. I would travel down to La Guardia, take a flight and it would land at some random airstrip, where we would collect Jacques. Only when we were safely in the air would he discuss matters directly. All of this meant he gave this one the absolute highest of priority.

"Because it was so extreme he had already sent an operative to live in La Paz, and make friends with the gardener. The old chef, as it turns out, was about to be fired, and so he saw a chance to get into the household and past the heavy security. One of his agents was a chef, and so he was flown in from Paris as a tourist, with credentials from a restaurant where Jacques knew the owner. He also had a false passport, all the normal things.

"I remember the conversation, and the journey as if it were yesterday ... "

The La Paz Assignment - June 1970

Living Amongst the Snakes

Jacques was agitated. It was extraordinarily unusual to see him like this, he was always a man of action. "This is the first time we cannot be absolutely certain the target is the guilty party," he says to Alan as they fly high over the skies of Illinois. "In my heart, I feel you HAVE found Bormann, but there is nothing incontrovertible that is linking him to the man in your vision. We are putting an operative in there, in his house, to collect hair samples. It is not foolproof, but as we have existing samples of his hair from Nazi files, if they do not marry up we know. If they do, then the likelihood is significantly higher."

"I have several men there now, one getting a position in one of his companies as an accountant. We must also track the money trail, as this will give us some definite clues. The old chef was fired last week for incompetence, and the man I have put in there is already hired. When the target heard a real French chef was in town, he dumped the old guy, which made our task easier. Our chef will collect the hair and he will also set up to record conversations. I have another man keeping tabs on the general comings and going via the gardener, and he is also researching everything to do with the man and anyone connected to him.

"Of course, none of these men know each other. None of them even know that there are others working on the same project. Now, this file (Jacques brings out a four-inch thick dossier) has everything known about Bormann and his associates. From what I have seen, yet to be confirmed, we may have indeed found one of the cruelest and the most elusive Nazi of them all. Wiesenthal has personally helped out on this one, and he had an incredible amount of detail on Bormann's suspected financials and the people he knows.

"If our man does tie this target into the Nazi Hunters files, if we see trading between him and the known parties in Bolivia and the rest of South America, then it is a very clear indication he is indeed at least a Nazi, if not Bormann himself. This is going to take some time, but Alan, as a side issue I note that you have not sent through any further visions. Is there a problem?"

Alan himself had wondered about this. "Maybe all of them over the last 25 odd years have been leading to this. I don't know. But for some reason, the well has run dry."

"Perhaps it is time, Alan. The cold reality is that the willingness of other parties to fund our operations has slowed to a trickle. This last effort will eat up all of the remaining funds, and it is only because of the significant interest in this case that we can draw enough cash for this program. But it is on a one-off basis. If it turns up to be a blind alley, then there is no more left to keep things running. If it turns out to accurate, there is still nothing left.

"And truth to tell, I am tired and need to retire." Jacques smiles, such a warm endearing face, you would trust your grandmother with this ruthless killer. "There comes a time for all of us, n'est pas? For this last mission, I am going to La Paz personally so I can coordinate this without the communications problems in and out of South America. But the real reason for this meeting, my friend? After all these years, this may be the very last time we meet."

Then Jacques paused, he deeply considered the next moment, and then added, "This operation, it will not be following the protocols. There are too many variables, and so because of this, I am willing to break with one more and invite you down, for what is likely to be the last target. Would you like to be with me in La Paz, Alan? Do you wish to be there for the closing of the curtain?"

Alan thinks of what he is booked to do, the classes he is to run, and then immediately discounts everything as secondary. For Twenty-Five years he has been the back-room driver of this project, and now he was being afforded an opportunity to walk into the sunlight to see how it all happens. How could he refuse? "What will I need to get?" he asked.

"Nothing," Jacques replied, with a huge grin. "Your false passport, clothes, everything you will need is on this plane, and we are already on the way in this fully-fuelled private jet. We stop to fill the tanks in Panama, and then we are straight to La Paz. You are going to be an integral part of this last operation."

Panama was not a matter of interest. They did not even leave the plane, and customs officers only gave them a cursory glance. They checked for overt weapons, drugs, but this was never really a problem for someone booked to go to Bolivia. A different story coming back. Jacques secretary had sent a quiet note through the Carlebach Gallery to his wife saying Alan had been called away on urgent business, she had received enough of those not to give it a moments thought.

La Paz was spectacular to fly into, the highest capital city in the world, with the extraordinary triple peak of Illimani dominating the scene in the background. A unique capital, in a land-locked country, and it appears, one of the last refuges for those few die-hards surviving at the end of the Nazi Empire. They book into a small, non-descript private hotel, the only paying guests by the look. La Casona, the inn where they stayed, was delightful. Its missionary bell tower marked the hotel's position in the Rosario district.

The paved courtyard surrounded a beautiful fountain, splashing water and giving a sense of cool in the dry heat of the mountain air.

Inside, it had typically Spanish high ceilings with exposed beams and extraordinary brick arch alcoves for reading spots. But the real surprise was the dining room, with a full brick dome, over sixty foot high. It was enormous, Alan felt you could have played a football game in there.

Jacques had not really said anything about the operation, other than that they would obtain each agent's information in their own time, and review the procedures on a daily basis. They spoke about many things, but never the reason they were there. Jacques had said prior to landing that his presence would arouse suspicion and that the story of two old friends on a site seeing tour was not going to be believed by anyone. Then he explained that the REAL reason they were there, flying in on a Jet owned by a wealthy Jew, arriving with a a man who was apparently an art historian, it was all designed to cause a flutter of consternation amongst the Nazi hiding out in Bolivia.

While they did not know of his covert activities, Jacques was well known as a man who tracked down assets once owned by Jews before WWII. It would be presumed that, as he brought a historian from the New York art scene with him, that he was tracking down stolen art works. Alan laughed, nothing the man did was by chance. He knew Alan could not resist the bait of coming to what may be the last act in this long running play, and every aspect of this staged show was calculated.

By stirring up the paranoia, lines of communications would be opened, letters and phone calls would be made, bribes would be paid. Their presence alone would stir the dormant pot and put every Nazi on edge, and nervous people make mistakes. The art of deception.

Carefully crafted meetings were being held in the ante-rooms of their hotel, with local art dealers being brought in, and asked about what was for sale, and Jacques had a list of unrecovered artwork he presented, saying he was interested in anything that led to him being able to find the present owners. Soon enough, no local art dealer would talk to them. Jacques smiled, day three in La Paz and the plan was working perfectly. "Next we talk to the tradesmen and gardeners, then the domestic servants, and we pay them for information. The local thugs will try to intimidate us next, and so I will have to hire a body guard."

Jacques was out with Alan in the soft evening light. The cool of dusk had a sharp edge here in the mountains, and a brisk walk was enlivening. "Now, obviously my bodyguard will just happen to be another one of my operatives. He will be the one who collects the information, and I will find my way to his rooms in secret. This will allow us to review intelligence without interruptions. Of course, our rooms are already bugged, and the owner of the hotel has already been paid not to allow others to stay here, so expect that everything the tradespeople and servants say will be recorded, and anything WE say to each other will also be noted.

"After the first meeting, anyone who comes to see us will be warned to stop. It will appear as if our purpose here is being frustrated, yet the real purpose is flushing out whoever is behind the local scene. If the fellow in your vision IS Bormann, it will be him, and there will be a tremendous increase in activity on his phone, with many more visitors turning up."

Alan smiled, Jacques was the leader of the Maquis for good reason. He understood these animals, he knew what they would do, and he was always a step ahead. "Do you think they will take direct action against us?"

"No, their only strength here is by being invisible. As long as they think they are winning, we will be left alone. And of course, everything we do here will be to make sure the real focus is not on our true purpose. We have the phone at the hacienda bugged, and not through the usual means. I have our man already in the house as the cook and he had tapped into the wires in the walls themselves and connected everything to a tape machine. Any call coming in triggers it to start recording, and it stops after the call hangs up, so it is completely invisible to the other parties on the phone.

"We do not try and bribe local officials who are already bribed. It would be a huge red flag to pay to have conversations to Roemer's house recorded at the exchange, however, I HAVE paid a Judge for a warrant for a totally different person. There is a German living here we do not suspect of war crimes but who we know is dealing in stolen art. Once more, distraction.

"Further, our man in the house is taking microfilm of every piece of correspondence. He can't open it, but he can photograph the address it came from, and we can look up the handwriting styles to see who it might be. Most of these Nazi write to each other in personal handwriting, they do not trust a secretary to type it. By tracking down WHO this Roemer is involved with, we will slowly build up the picture, and make certain he is the target we think he is."

Fascism is not defined by the number of its victims, but by the way it kills them.

Jean-Paul Sartre

At The Roemer House

Piecing Together the Facts

Carl Roemer was thoroughly enjoying the new cook. Proper French cuisine, such a delight, and such luck to find this man passing through. Of course, he had been vetted, but the credentials held up. His former employer had personally vouched for him and confirmed that he left for a tour of Bolivia. The man was also tested after he applied for the job, to make sure he could cook the house specialties from his last employment. And it was delightful.

Of course, it was also a little expensive, but worth every penny. Proper croissants, proper pastries. and the little things, chicken bathed in an almond pastry, with sesame and ginger oil. The locals had no idea. He almost felt like he was back in Europe. Roemer sighed, so much he missed, but this was the cost of things. Dammit, not another call. Those irritating fools in town were starting to really annoy him.

He picks up the phone, annoyed his afternoon repast has been interrupted, "Yes?" he says tersely. Expecting yet another laborious report from some paranoid local about who the French dog was speaking to now, but he is pleasantly surprised to hear the polite voice of the police superintendent. This meant news.

"Senor," the inspector says in his broken German, "We have an interest for you. One of your friends is being spied on, in regards his art buying activities. All properly applied for, unfortunately, and legal, but I felt it was important for you to be kept informed, as you have asked."

"Yes Inspector, the news is greatly appreciated. And now we know, I need you to do exactly nothing. Do not approach the Frenchman, do not have either of them brought in on any charge. We will feed them false information and they will chase their tails on red herrings. Thank you." And he goes back to his lunch with Gusto. These stupid people coming in, don't they understand there is a network in place to deal with them. The Germans here have stayed under the radar for decades, and will continue to do so.

Even if they found a painting, what would they do? Approach the Police to have someone arrested? The very notion was laughable, these stupid Jews and Jew lovers imagining they would get one over a true-blood German. He finished his lunch, then signalled for Consuelo. She was a nice thing. Pretty, which meant she looked Spanish and not like the ugly little Indians creatures that were all over Bolivia.

She walks into the room, meekly undoes her dress, and lays down face forward on the bed. She takes it like a good girl should, but of course, if there were trouble her children living with their Grandmother would suffer. He had made it clear to her what was expected, and the consequences of failure. It pays to ensure loyalty, and these half-wit creatures have to be pressed into honesty. Thieving little pigs, every one of them. But he would sleep well today, good news, good news indeed.

Consuelo, of course, detested Roemer. She was little more than a dog in this household, but the new Chef seemed to understand. He was a charming, courteous man who spoke to her in Spanish, not the guttural German of her employer. She was a university educated woman who spoke four languages, but instead of the high profile position as a translator she had expected, her filthy step-father, one of Roemer's friends, had insisted she work here.

She had been married, her husband died running tours up the mountain, and she had children to raise. This job meant security, the boy and the girl would stay with her mother, and she would send money home for their education. There was little choice, really, and the conditions of providing sex at the time meant nothing to her. Her step-father had always had his way, his friends also. Sometimes all together, so this was preferable because it was just one of them. Roemer would not share because he feared disease.

But this charming middle-aged French man who spoke her native Spanish. He did not judge her. Yes, of course he understood what the arrangement was, but he did not judge her. She heard the snoring, and knew it was safe to speak openly with him. "He liked the croissants in particular. I am sure he is very happy with you here." Then she noted, as she got to the kitchen, that he was cleaning up. So lovely, someone with respect. She didn't have to do everything.

Jean-Paul smiled a warm and genuinely friendly smile. He liked this girl, he felt for her. It had only been two weeks since he took up the position, but already he had heard enough in the recordings to know this man was a Nazi. They all had the same arrogance. Roemer was all smiles and courtesy towards himself, of course. He knew full well the impossibility of finding a proper French Chef in Bolivia, and fortunately the man was so paranoid he had no-one come for dinners. As chef, he did the odd lunch, but nothing extravagant was called for. In truth, the job itself was a cakewalk. The tapes he took out on his person every day, mini-cassettes that he put in a small plastic bag and pushed up his butt. It would not pay to be searched and be found with incriminating evidence.

In many ways, the job was all too easy. He arrived at ten a.m. left at seven-thirty p.m. and stayed down the way in a rooming house. He was paid very well for a servant in Bolivia, so he could quite enjoy himself, and he made sure he did. No action could arouse suspicion, so while he was not a drinker, (no assassin in Jacques employ was) he would go to the bars, talk with the men, check out the girls, and be back in his bed by eleven p.m. Six days a week, Sundays off.

He would prepare and serve lunch, and then while Roemer was sexing the girl he could do many of the secret things that were needed. While he slept, the girl always went out to her own quarters in the yard, feeding the dogs as she did so. The dogs, trained German Shepherds, were good with him now but there was no doping them. They would only take food from the girl or Roemer.

Electrical fencing all round the yard, with alarm systems that lit up and howled if anything was tripped. To add to the complication, all doors and windows were locked as he left and the girl was always sent back to her own shack. The man was entirely alone every night. He trusted no one, and not so much as a hooker ever came to visit after hours. During the day, he had set appointments, and from his office there was a clear view of any car that turned up. Roemer had to recognize it before he opened the electronic gates, which was done via a switch in his desk.

The girl did the cleaning of everything but the pistols and rifles, which Roemer kept in a locked room. Every afternoon when he woke, he would take one or two, and clean them. Jean-Paul (the chef) was never shown these, but he knew from long experience what each one was, just from the sound of the bolt unlocking, or a barrel being cocked. Enough to understand the man had a small arsenal up there.

Men arrived at set times for many and varied reasons. They would leave, their conversations duly recorded through the telephone trip switch he had set up in the pantry. After he returned home, he would listen to the tapes. The conversations were always in German and were mostly about mining, harvest on some farm, or a labor dispute. But since "the boss" had arrived it all hotted up. He was pleased to note that in the last week almost every call was regarding how to hide their paintings and art till the "French Pig" left. (That was their unsubtle code-word for Jacques)

Good, the subterfuge was working. It was now only a matter of time before the hair analysis was done and they would know if they had their man. But Jean-Paul knew in his bones that they did.

Jacques had not told him who it was, saying this is what they were needing to resolve before taking action, but Jean-Paul knew a Nazi when he smelt one, and this one stank of Hitler. He even had a damn Swastika in his office. He hoped the evidence would come soon, and be the confirmation what he hoped it would be.

He would truly enjoy dispatching this son of a bitch.

The Accountant

Doing the Numbers

Raoul was one of the last remaining Maquis from the Spanish war. He found himself quite enjoying Bolivia, and was very happy he had accepted the assignment. A forensic accountant by trade, now retired, he was quite well off. But then the offer of an all expenses paid holiday in Bolivia, one where he got paid by the target for doing what he loved! It was a fantastic offer, and brought him out for one last Nazi hunt. He loved hunting down these bastards financials and ruining them.

Of course, to the Germans running things, bringing in an independent accountant with the impeccable reputation of Raoul Mendez was a small coup. It meant they could track down some issues they knew they were having, but which their own number crunchers were not finding.

It was a contact at the American Embassy, of all places, who had suggested the Spaniard as a way to help them with their problems in Bolivia, saying the man had cracked a number of theft rings in the past.

Roemer Mining Administration was set up in a valley that took a solid day of four wheel driving to get to from town. It was just 120 miles North of La Paz, but it was slow going. However, the gold made everything else insignificant. Plus the difficult road had the reverse benefit of making it much harder for anyone loaded with gold to get out.

Raoul had arrived some weeks earlier, to a place called Teoponte. The town itself, was no great cultural wonder, but the people were friendly, the food was good, and for a few dollars he could live in luxury at a local monastery. It was apparently a situation set up for VIP workers from Europe who worked at the mine from time to time.

In any gold mine there is always an abject fear of theft. Naturally, the Germans never fully trusted their mine managers or their local accountants, and they had paid big money to get him here. His job was to scrutinize every single transaction and find out where leakage or theft was happening.

The very first day of the job, the grovelling, compliant mine manager was caught out. The man thought he could bribe Raoul to turn a blind eye. Most men would have happily accepted the bonus, but even if he were not on the job for a far different reason, he would have still turned the thieving little bastard in. The manager had been creating a rake by charging the miners "protection". Effectively, pay me or you are fired, with the extorted income he got being written up as an insurance.

Big, blonde Germans turned up as soon as he filed the report at the end of the week, and they beat the crap out of the man. Everyone at the mine heard it, just as everyone knew what he had been doing. More importantly, it meant was that he was "in" as a trusted employee. The mine administration now gave him every little thing he asked for, and this was not just for the Gold mine. He had open access to ALL of the information in their files.

After he had been there a month he was quite settled in. Raoul had gotten himself a nice little girlfriend, basically a hooker, but she was happy to be with him each evening, and the monks appeared not to notice her. In all, he quite liked the whole story, and absolutely was enjoying himself. More to the point, he had turned up absolute proof of a financing program for all Germans in South America. This little Gold Mine had far reaching tentacles, and it all centered around a man called Roemer in La Paz. This individual was essentially bank rolling a large number of projects right across the continent.

The real news, and the reason he presumed Jacques asked him to come here, was that the gold mined and the money lent out via gold as a security did not correlate. He was fairly certain that the flunkies who threw all their files at him had no idea, otherwise, they would have been more circumspect, but they weren't. Now the simple arithmetic of gold produced over the value per ounce loaned out showed a huge gap between what the mine produced and the amount of finance the business was offering.

Yes, it was a rich little gold mine, but not even half of what was being lent out to a hundred different companies was being met by the actual turnover. And in every case in South America, it meant stolen gold being run through a paper trail to clean it up. This mine was a laundry.

But his report to Jacques was clear. The Roemer Mining was a hub for literally thousands of transactions, with connections to what seemed like every German who was in business in South America. It was BIG, and someone, somewhere, was tipping in vast amounts of capital to make it bigger. The gold the mine was trading was twice what it produced, so where was it coming from?

Directly from Roemer and his associates, it would seem. Every significant contact he saw was written was signed by him or his lieutenant. All of this went down in his workbook in a way that looked like he was merely keeping track of transactions. In the end, he had a pile of books, though only one had the real information Jacques needed. It took almost six weeks, but he finally finished the task and delivered his findings to the mine's offices in la Paz. Naturally, the important book was left under the seat of his car, where it was quietly collected.

There was a great consternation amongst the various directors as he announced his discoveries. SO many fingers had gotten into the pie with the leaking cash adding up to millions, and they had been utterly clueless. He knew businessmen, he lived with them all his life, and all these people were amateurs. No real manager of a business would have allowed so many things to have gone unnoticed.

The Directors had absolutely no idea how much money was sitting in bad debts, unclaimed receipts, nor how much was taken from that old chestnut, the petty cash drawer. Always, every single time, office staff would be rorting the petty cash for beer money, but when it came to thousands of companies, the cost of this alone climbed into the hundreds of thousands every year. As he loved to say, it was not-so-petty cash.

Every single one of the men in the various directorships, the men that controlled so much of the local and South American economy, were German. They spoke in German, they even thought like old fashioned German's. And you could see on their faces how they truly believed themselves to be the Masters and the South Americans the slaves. Which naturally meant that so many of the 'slaves' went out of their way to stick it to their employers.

The accountant returned back to Valencia a significantly wealthier man, both in assets and information. So many Nazis he had found, that even he was astonished. Jacques would be kept busy for quite some time finding out their true history. But the ONE that stood out above and beyond all others, the one who was not there at the meeting, but the man who was behind everything, Carl Roemer.

By deduction, so much unaccounted for wealth meant it was stolen. The facts spoke for themselves: A Gold Mine that lent vast sums of money using Gold as security, added to the fact it was controlled by a single man operating the entire venture, this equaled a thief. Every main player was clearly German, and clearly ex-military by the look of them. None of them real businessmen. This whole place reeked of stolen Nazi gold, and a lynchpin from the old regime was organizing it.

Raoul hated the Nazi. He also hated with a passion businessmen who were sloppy and arrogant. Here he found both, and more than this, he had posted off to his old office a complete list of all the companies this lot were working with in Europe. There, as a forensic accountancy firm, the staff would quietly ask questions of each supplier or purchaser of Roemer Mining goods. He laughed, one by one he would quietly communicate to these clients using the South American gold that it was really stolen Nazi gold. *Gold from the teeth of the Jews they exterminated.* It would take years, but Raoul knew that, in time, he would bankrupt them all.

NOTE: in 1980, ten years after this event, the Bolivian Government nationalized the Gold Fields North of La Paz.

The Gardener

Tracking the Arrogant via the Most Humble

The small, athletic Frenchman enjoyed this old gardener. They both liked to pedal their bikes and on Sundays, the fellows free day, they went for miles up and down the winding roads outside of the capital. This was how Pierre gained the little guys trust. Over the last six weeks he had been extracting from Stephan, the gardener, the details of who came in and out of Roemer's compound. This was by asking about the cars he had to fix (Stephan was also the resident mechanic) and who owned them.

The German's were addicted to their Mercedes, especially the "presidential" limousines. The big 6.3 litre Pullman at the Roemer house was quite the show stealer. Every business associate that visited came out to see this magnificent vehicle, and tracking down these men was his real job here. His task: *find all those connected to Roemer, log their art and possessions.* He was piecing together the names, addresses, and details of every German in La Paz, seeing what they had, and after that working out what stolen Nazi wealth they enjoyed.

Simple, astute questioning of the Roemer gardener every Sunday revealed who had turned up. Pierre's cover story as a buyer of rare species of flora meant he could gather a list of who had what species in their gardens fairly easily. His real task was to gather a secret list of what notable things an individual owner had locked up in his house. The right questions, and the locals talked openly.

All of the Germans here had locked compounds, electric fences, and scared servants. However, they all also had a gardener, and little Stephan here, he knew all of them and gave Pierre a personal introduction. Given the contact information for all the local gardeners then meant he could meet them individually and quietly extract information. His simple ploy to get in was the search for rare species. Pierre knew his plants. By quietly talking to them about the price he was prepared to pay for certain botanicals, he got their trust. And when he had their trust, quiet questions about what was in each of those houses revealed what he needed to know.

Statues, art, these were but one thing he cataloged. The secret gold was to be found in the peculiarities of the home owners. So many of these Germans had specialized collections, dolls, stamps, miniature Victorian art, and by identifying who collected what they could track this information back to known Nazis who had a fetish for that specific thing. This linked a person to their past far more than any photo, and was as conclusive as a finger print for identifying someone.

He had already retrieved the financials book for Jacques, under the seat of the car as directed. He would not normally look inside, but a note from the boss had asked him to correlate the names in the book with what he has discovered. Jacques wanted to know if it matched what the Germans had at their properties, and in particular, to list the hobbies and collections of each individual in the financials book specifically. He wanted a summary of both hobbies and assets, a task which kept him busy all week. Now he had the file completed and was out pedaling his bicycle with the Gardener, going to an agreed spot high in the hills outside of town.

After all these years of snooping around Nazis, even he was surprised at what he found. They had SO much damn money here, and suffered absolutely no risk. It was not hard to find out which government officials and Police were taking bribes. It was common knowledge with most of the locals. You just had to sit in a bar and ask questions, and they talked about how corrupt everything was, and who was to blame.

"Stephan, we need to pull over and have a drink. This looks like a nice park." The old gardener smiles, it would seem these French are not so fit, but he laughs and they have a small repast and some water, sitting there looking out over the town far below them. "It's a good place," says Pierre. "So many do not have as comfortable a life as what we find here."

Stephan was normally a man of few words. He preferred his garden to speak for him and enjoyed being alone creating the small things of beauty to offset some of the horrors of the past. But today he suddenly got talkative. "It is true, but as a native, we see the harsh side of things, not just the pretty pictures of progress. Take my employer, for instance, Roemer came here in 1946, bought the Gold Mine, and set up in his compound. My father worked for him for a decade before he got too old, and I took his place.

"But did Roemer give my father one extra penny for his retirement? No. Nothing, not even a thank you. Does he walk about the garden and say how beautiful it is? No, not once. And the reason is simple, he does not care. He considers me a necessary burden, but acceptable because I keep his cars running. The garden is for show, something that looks good to others, and which makes things tidy. That is all he is interested in, the fact that it is tidy.

"If a scrap of paper blows in, he will abuse me. I had nothing to do with it, but his yard is untidy, therefore it is my fault. He is an ugly man, Pierre, so many of these Germans are ugly men. You will have heard the same story from my friends who I sent you to see. They all despise their employers. They are men without souls." The gardener sat quietly. It was rare for him to speak so openly, but he found himself trusting this old Frenchman who loved the rare and unusual plants here in Bolivia.

Pierre said nothing. He had already taped the package under the seat without anyone noticing, which was the real reason they were here, but he heard the old man, and he understood. He wanted to say "They SOLD their Souls," but he bit his lip. Instead, he said, "But what do we care, the garden grows, we have something we have created that has beauty. If a dog cannot smell the rose, it is not the fault of the rose."

The little Bolivian said nothing, but nodded, and enjoyed the beautiful light of the late afternoon. In the fading tones of eventide, they make their way back to town, rolling along at an easy rate. "Come," says Pierre, "Let me buy you dinner. (He waves down the objection) Nothing fancy, let's just have something nice. I may not be here much longer and I want you to only have good memories of my visit."

Of course, if what Pierre suspected was the case, that the man's employment may soon come to an end because his employer has suffered chronic and permanent blood loss, then this old man would soon be out of work.

He made sure he had the correct mailing details for his family, and when he returned home, he would sell some off the rare species he had collected here and send the money to Stephan. It would be enough for him to live comfortably for many years. The man deserved no less.

the fine art of - *alan wood-thomas*

Fascist Reunion

Gathering of the Clan

Roemer was not one for impromptu get-together's, but for this turn of events, he made an exception. He moved forward the yearly meeting of the Nazis because his men had managed to stymie the French dog at every turn. And now, they were heading home with nothing. After four weeks all the pair found were dead ends. He had the entire La Paz crew here now, and he broke out a bottle of Châteaux Rothschild just for the occasion.

"Yes Mien Obergruppenführer, it is true. I have seen the flight plans lodged, the pilot has prepared the plane. The pair will fly out tomorrow, and good riddance to them." Oberführer Rienz was one of his operatives who kept track of everyone and everything. The man clipped his heels together and gave the Nazi salute.

Roemer looked him over. A good lad, a credit to his father. Fine Aryan blood, strong straight nose, blond hair, blue eyes, and he worked out. He was fit. If only they had more like him. "Good work everyone. We have beaten off yet another Jewish plot to take what is rightfully ours. But let us not pretend this is over. There will be more, and we must remain vigilant, and prepared.

"In particular, I want not one of you to be found slacking off with the disciplines. Never sleep in the same room two nights running. Make sure your guard dog is trained to take food only from yourself or a trusted servant. Make certain you have a loaded weapon by your bed at all times. We know they are out to get us, the filthy Maquis.

"Every month we hear of another brother who had fallen, cowardly slain in their bed, their throats cut. Do not allow this to be you! To this end, I have had fashioned protective equipment specifically for when you are asleep." And with this, Roemer brings out a flexible, wide collar. "This wraps around your neck and has layers of surgical steel mesh running across it. If someone tries to use a knife, they will not be cutting your neck. And you know, if there is anything strange in your room, anything at all, take your gun and shoot it.

"We have lost too many men in the last few years, too many good men. Rienz's father for one, that was a terrible blow to his family, but at least the son had stood up to become one of the true warriors. (nodding to Rienz) You have done an excellent job on these visitors, I must add. All of you, of course, but particularly our newest recruit. You anticipated every turn they would make, and cut them off from all useful information."

Roemer offers his glass in a toast, "To the Fuhrer!"

"To the Fuhrer" they all echoed back, drinking down the glass of champagne.

"Well, we have won this round, we will win the next, and the one after. But only if we stay united, only if we keep control of our affairs and stay hidden and under the radar. If you need advice, come and see me. And look about you, this house is the perfect example of how to set yourselves up. Electric fencing, gate control from inside the house. Minimal staff and I have an ax over the head of any locals that work for me. Remember! It is all about order and control." Roemer paused, let the message sink in, then gave his usual speech.

"Men, it has been many years since the disgusting communists destroyed our homeland, and we cannot go back. But we must keep our ideals alive, we must educate our children in the right and proper ways to retain both their position in society and their dignity. Do not forget for one moment that any one of these lustful natives would happily kill you for your wallet, so be on guard at all times.

"But now, a far happier occasion, we have a lunch made for us by my new and very genuine French Chef. I collected him a few weeks ago. He costs me a fortune, but after today I think you will all agree, he is worth it!" And laughing and cheering, they made their way to the formal dining room, where a magnificent luncheon had been prepared.

Consuelo served the meals, of course, not looking up or catching the eye of any of those filthy men who were eying her as she walked around. She hated these yearly gatherings, and this one came early. Well, with luck, they would all leave early as well.

The Sums are Added, the Debt is Due

Connecting the Dots

No information ever went back to their hotel where they stayed. Jacques had a room several blocks away booked for their 'bodyguard' and had a second key to access it. The man had been used by him in the past and was reliable. He is the one who went out and collected the packages, the microfilm, and the cassettes, so that all Jacques had to do was to make sense out of it.

To get the information he dressed as the bodyguard, and that man, chosen in part for the similarity he had to Jacques in height and build, was ensconced in the Frenchman's room, apparently asleep. Alan and himself had only been here for four weeks, yet by the transcripts of conversations he read (from the tapping of the phones at the Roemer house) the general consensus was that that they had become very frustrated by their lack of results, and were going home empty-handed.

After the information was combed through, it was self-evident where stolen treasures were hiding. There was a lot of contraband and not all of it from WWII! These people were actively collecting stolen art from all around the world. Jacques laughed, and of course to collect this he by-passed the corrupt local government agencies completely and went direct to his friends at the American Embassy. Upon his suggestion they would send out CIA operatives who would happen to 'discover' the works in various houses, to be done soon after they left La Paz.

And what could the Germans do? Nothing. The art and sculptures were on the international list of stolen works, and though no one was going to prosecute the remnants of the Nazi here, they would at least lose extensive and quite valuable assets. He would be able to claim the reward, and offset some of their costs here, from the relative insurance agencies. Of course, he had already obtained letters of writ from a number of insurance companies giving him permission to source stolen items. This had all been arranged before he left Europe, and calling in the CIA was standard practice here in South America. They took their cut, of course. Overall, this had been a very expensive investigation in La Paz, far more than usual, but well worth it.

The picture was clear. Roemer's business connections were all ex-Nazi. All of them were as soaked in guilt as their leader, and now they were known and identified (for the most part) he would hand this information over to Wiesenthal. The expense and grind of dealing with the law courts in the various countries is a slow and painful torture, but the Jews were past masters at it. They would make sure this lot suffered for the crimes, one way or another. Providing all theser names with the information to Wiesenthal was the substance of the deal he made for the Bormann file.

There was no question left in his mind. The had found Hitler's secretary. Every associate had some connection back to Bormann, and though the man himself had clearly gone through plastic surgery to alter his face, and despite the fact that he regularly washed his finger prints with acid to make sure he had none, the evidence was clear. When your best friend in the Reich had a model train fetish and some unique and special carriages, then someone looking like that same man, with those same carriages, now lives here in La Paz! Well, enough of these associations tell you the story.

It was also clear he was financing his operations here with Nazi Gold. The most likely reason he bought a gold mine would have been to cover this up. The work of the accountant, when cross referenced with the original operative, Pierre, who had tracked down the information through the various gardeners, this proved the financial connections. The stolen art works discovered in the various houses of these former Nazis was damning and conclusive proof of collusion.

Hair analysis had come back. It was a match, and while this on its own was not absolute proof, when married to the evidence, the associations, and the military organization, this was clearly a high ranking Nazi. The fact it was Bormann himself just made the job so much sweeter.

His close listening to the tapes was what finally confirmed Jacques suspicions. Roemer had the distinct accent from the district where Bormann was born. Also, the man dealt with people over the phone like a Nazi very used to giving orders, but more than this: he would use information in such a way, so as to manipulate the men about him into doing exactly what he wanted them to. Just as Bormann did when he was Hitler's secretary.

So few seemed to understand the obvious. Hitler was only able to do an achieve the evils he did because of men like this. His secretary was not just assisting, he was instrumental in constructing so many of the deepest evils of the Third Reich.

He closed the file. This one he could not burn, it was far too important. Bormann would need to be positively identified for him to claim the reward, and all the evidence must be there. Well, in this instance he would just have the bodyguard stuff it into his baggage before it went onto the jet.

He wrote a list of instructions for the chef, to be collected when he went to get supplies. Essentially, Roemer/Bormann was NOT to die in his bed. He was to end his life well away from the house, thus dispelling suspicion on Jean-Paul or innocent members of the household. This meant something would have to be staged at the Mine that required the man's personal attention. So they will need a slow acting poison, something that does not show its effect for a day or so. A simple inquiry to Pierre days earlier had found the right poison, a powdered form of Death Cap.

Getting the instructions to Jean-Paul was the next step, which was as simple as a shopping list left in a prearranged book at the store where he bought supplies.

It was all in code, of course. *'Mushrooms for the trip to the mine'* was so simple. Because Alan had seen mushroom soup in his vision, they chose this as the key word for poison. *'Trip to the mine'* meant away from the house, and the only place the target went outside of town was to his mine. Putting the two together meant Roemer/Bormann was to be poisoned, and the bottle of truffle extract Jean-Paul collected had been thoroughly laced with it.

The other main consideration, they will need the body to confirm the kill, which meant they had to get it out of Bolivia. There was a hefty reward for Bormann, and all players in this final scene, and those still remaining, would need a pension payment as thank you for their work. Obviously, the situation here was that this man Roemer was revered and he had his own funerary arrangements in place that must be abided by.

Well, this simply meant they knew where the body would be. As it was not likely he was going to do a Jesus and get up out of his tomb, the solution was to wait a few weeks, then break into Bormann's mausoleum, swap in a substitute body, and take the original. Not the most pleasant of tasks, but nothing that they haven't had to do in the past.

The innocents. The Consuelo girl, she may well be blamed, or at least be suspected. (The local police don't need evidence to convict anyone of a crime) She has children, she can't hide or run. Making someone pay for their ruthless injustice to others cannot be at the expense of injustice to an innocent party, but there seemed no easy solution. He would have to arrange for her to be away for a week, and so not connected to any investigation that would follow. And there WILL be an investigation.

Bormann had enormous assets, but as Roemer there were no children or relatives to pass these along to. It was going to be a huge fight, as all the local Germans go for each other's throats to get a piece of the pie. It would have been fun to stay and watch, all of them killing each other for gold.

But for now, the plan was set. Bormann will die by poison at the hand of his prized French Chef. Jacques set out the instructions for his agents, always in code, and left it under the table cloth for his bodyguard to find and distribute. And that would seem to be that.

It all had the sense of an ending: The closing of the night, the shutting down of the journey. After twenty five years Alan had had no more visions, nothing for three months now. It would also seem that all Alan's work to date was leading up to this one core Nazi.

When Bormann dies, when the unfindable, untraceable one dies, all of them, every Nazi in hiding in South America will sit up at night, unable to sleep, wondering, *'Will I be next?'*.

It will look like he died from food poisoning or a flu, but they KNOW how many wanted Bormann dead. But who organised it? Someone must have caved in, and taken a pile of cash for giving out the information.

Paranoia is corrosive. It destroys any trust you have in your associates and breaks down any intimacy you might have felt with loved ones. A disgruntled wife leaves you, your children don't want to know the strange man who is their father, and slowly the acid of fear and corruption eats away your inner vitals. The person delivering the telegram, he could be the assassin sent to get you. The man looking at you oddly as you walk through town, he could be an assassin.

Over 300 Nazis lost their lives over the last quarter of a century because of Alan's visions. Odd, it matched the number of Nazis who were actually locked up in 1947. Jacques had a chuckle to himself. Had they done enough? Had they put the fear of death into enough of these scum to ensure the evil of Nazi Germany never rises again?

For now, it was time to leave Bolivia, deliver Alan back to his family, and let the process unfold. When they leave the country, Bormann will relax, and this will make Jean-Paul's task much easier. It was going to end up being a job well done.

When the rich [and politically powerful] make war, it's the poor [and politically weak] who die.

Jean-Paul Sartre

Panama Bound

Flying Home

Alan knew this was the last journey. The connection with Jacques was the longest single friendship he had in his life, the man was more a brother than anything else. And yet, it was a business partnership. The 'profit' was purely the satisfaction that came from serving life, but it was still a business. The visions had ceased, and while he missed the excitement, he now could focus on just being what he was. No more secrets, no more double life.

Bormann was the final and most important target, and it was fitting he should be the last. But he felt mixed emotions: It was the passing of an era, and the loss of a friend because he knew that with his arrival back in New York, that this would put an end to his relationship with Jacques. Not just the Frenchman himself, but the Maquis, and everything else of that original, secret life he started at age sixteen.

A jumbled bag of images flowed through his thoughts: Spain, leaving France, New York, marriage, children, art ... Yet everything had been secondary to his true purpose, ending the Nazi threat. It was like a retirement without the gold watch, or anyone congratulating you, or anyone even knowing. The invisible Assassin was no more.

Both men went through the checks at Panama, then Jacques said he needed to stop over for the night, so they booked a room. A rare occasion, but in general anonymity they ate together in public, chatted about old times, had a wine, and went out for a walk in the sultry evening air. Slowly they wound their way to the Miraflores Locks, looking at the ships steaming through from the Pacific to the Atlantic and vice versa.

"This place is a symbol of the new world." Jacques spoke as they stood in the moonlight. "It is where industrial might and human will combined to conquer nature, or at least this is what some believe. The truth is, profit drove this project. Money is the God now, and this canal, this city (he waves at Panama City) exists because of this pursuit for money.

"It is places like this that truly harbor the Nazi and their kind. They have the laws that permit anything, as long as the money flows, and the bribes are paid. Nothing we have done will change this, Alan. I feel a sense of loss, a sense of shame for humanity itself. This is not why we stopped here overnight, of course, I have a little business to attend to. The plane will take you back to New York in the morning, I will not be on it."

"This is the final farewell, then?" Alan asked, though he already knew the answer. Their business together had been a journey from 1937 to 1970, thirty-three years. But the very nature of this work meant an informal friendship was not possible. They were brothers in a covert war, a secret war, and there would be no reunion gatherings, no talk of time in the trenches. When he left, they were done.

Jacques breathed in. "I will remain here for a few months. The body of Bormann needs to be dealt with, and proof given to Wiesenthal. You will receive a check for your share of the reward, and yes (he waves his hand) I know no-one did this for the money, but cash IS the new reality. For myself, I have nothing to go back to in France, despite my love for her, so I will be traveling to Australia and living out my days there in peace, well away from all former connections.

"When this door shuts, Alan, I do not want it re-opening for any reason. The Jews will take up the lists we got from Bolivia, and there is extensive work to be done, assets to be recovered, guilty parties to be brought before a judge, and all this consumes time and energy that I no longer have. Presuming all goes well in La Paz, this is the fitting Coup-de-Gras to our mutual employment."

"You are retiring completely, then?" Alan asked.

"Well, perhaps not quite yet. There is a little matter here involving transferring ownership of this canal to the Americans. It is only fair, they built it. But this last endeavor will pay for my retirement. There are a few greedy men who need to be educated, and I am part of the process of organizing this. In part, it is payment for all the Americans have done to help us over the years."

Jacques laughs at the look of surprise on Alan's face. "Yes, Alan. A great deal of assistance was given to us by your Government, in the back ground, of course. Your CIA was as interested in removing the threat posed by Nazi officers in third world countries as we were in balancing the scales of justice for the ones so wronged.

"And you will also be repaid, in ways that are not overt. Commissions will come, plus, something worth more than gold, you will be left alone and not interfered with."

Jacques stopped, held out his hand, and took Alan's right hand in both of his. "Thank you, Alan Wood-Thomas. Without you, well, who knows what we would have done." Alan places his right hand over both of Jacques, they take a firm grip and hold for a moment. Then a black limousine pulls up, and Jacques says, "You know your way back to the hotel. Your proper passport is there, and a car will take you to the airport at 9 a.m. Breakfast is paid for, the room is paid for. I will maybe see you in the next life."

And he was gone.

The Final Solution

Death to the Nazi

Jean-Paul felt the tension easing from the house in La Paz. Jacques had left, and the extreme activity over the phone lines had dropped off. He was to await one final call before disconnecting everything and moving forward to the task he came here for. And now, just ten days on from the departure of the Master of the Dance, which is how he thought of Jacques, the phone rang. It was the manager from the Mine. A disaster, it needed Roemer's personal attention.

The call was timed to come late in the afternoon, so Roemer could not leave immediately. As it was, the man was visibly strained. He hated leaving his compound, and when Jean-Paul asked what he would like for his supper, he said, "Just coffee and maybe some of that excellent Mushroom soup you do." The chef nodded, so much courtesy he received from this man, yet he saw how he treated the locals so cruelly. They were dogs to him, dogs to be used, abused, then disposed of.

And how fitting, he asks for the thing written up in the original vision, the Mushroom Soup. He had been given the perfect tool, the poison mushroom compound that would find its way in there, it was an extraordinary poison. There was little to no great effect for twelve hours, then it caused a slow, three-day spiral into what seemed a terrible flu, after which it killed you through liver and kidney failure. A pity he would not be there to see it. "How long do you think you will be away?" Jean-Paul asked.

"At least a week by the sound of it. I will leave notice at my office in town when I am returning, and they will contact you.."

"So a week hiking in the mountains will not be a problem, then?"

"Take ten days. This will be a messy, protracted affair."

"Very good Sir, and what would you like to take with you for traveling? Might I suggest I stay up late this evening and prepare some cakes, pastries and croissants for you, to help soften the burden and strain of the journey?"

Roemer, whom Jean-Paul now understood to be Martin Bormann, Hitler's personal secretary, smiled warmly. "You see, this is the difference between we Europeans and those Indian dogs out here: Culture, intelligence, and consideration. Yes that would be truly appreciated, and please do not be concerned, even though you are not here, I will ensure your wages are still paid."

Jean-Paul bowed, and left to prepare everything for his journey. He knew this was about to happen because Consuelo had received an emergency telegram just the day before, saying that her father was about to die. She had gotten the week off, without pay, of course. This was to be the trigger, so without further ado, he prepared the soup, but oddly enough, this time Roemer came down to have supper with his Chef. Very unusual.

In the middle of his preparations of food for the following day, Roemer had decided to come and chat. He never did this, but Jean-Paul presumed as the servants were all gone, the man simply wanted to talk to another European. The reality, Roemer was beyond lonely. He was completely isolated here in Bolivia. His family thought he was dead, his country thought he was dead. No one cared about him, and his fate was to die in this foreign land away from the fatherland he loved. This French Chef was his only real and immediate link back to Europe.

"Will you have some soup with me?" he asked, charming, benign, and unusually friendly.

Jean-Paul had to stop a rising panic. Did the man suspect? "Ah, I would love to." And he takes a small taste, closing his eyes, saying, "Delightful. I love mushrooms so much, but unfortunately, they repeat quite awfully on me. Always have, ever since I was a child. Even truffles, you know. Can you imagine the suffering of a French Chef not being able to eat his favorite ingredient?" Then he brightened, and reaching into his pantry, "And I almost forgot! You reminded me, only yesterday I found the most wonderful reminder of Europe here in La-Paz. A truffle power imported from the South of France, here in Bolivia, can you believe? It makes the perfect condiment to the soup, n'est pas?"

Roemer smiles warmly. His suspicious were immediately relieved when the chef was happy to taste the food. And Truffle power... delightful! "How come you have not used this before?" He asks.

Jean-Paul laughs, "Ah, it turned up when I was last shopping. I could not believe my eyes, it is one of my secret ingredients that I used in France, and there it was in the local supply store. It must be added right as the soup is served." And with this he ladles the mushroom soup into a fine porcelain bowl, adding the poison that was already laced into the truffle power, along with a few croutons that were dosed with a barbiturate. Roemer digests his meal happily, extolling the virtues of European culture and refinement, and saying how much he appreciated Jean-Paul.

"I will bottle some of this soup for you to take as well, Sir. It is not quite the same reheated, but it will still be better than any of the slop they serve up at the mine."

"Excellent!" says Roemer, delighted that his suspicions have been allayed. Obviously, there can be no problem if the man is going to let him take the soup with him. He didn't know WHY he suddenly became paranoid, but in the past it usually proved correct. The CIA battering in the doors of his business associates the other day, stealing all their art, it had affected him quite badly, and put him on edge.

That damn French dog had gotten one over on them, and he hated him. But what else did the man discover? Roemer started seeing shadows and phantoms everywhere, but here, thank God, in his own house all was in order.

And that night, Hitler's secretary slept soundly for the first time in years. There was something incredibly calming in that soup, and he most surely would be taking it with him tomorrow.

As Roemer/Bormann slept the sleep of a drugged man, Jean-Paul carefully removed any and all evidence of his phone tapping. As the baking came to a close, he packed up the dead man's lunch and travel goods, and left a carefully written note about the things the kitchen would need when his employer returned.

It was done. He collected all the equipment in his backpack, and left for his room, and the further cleaning up of any evidence that might be found there. It was unlikely he would be a suspect, because he expected that 'the French Chef' would be considered as dead as Bormann inside a few days.

Tomorrow he would be seen on the slopes of Mount Illimani, traveling on his own on some adventure to a remote area of the mountain. At that time of year, accidents were incredibly common, and the room he had booked for nine days would never be slept in.

Jean-Paul, the French Chef, would soon be just another statistic, in a long line of unaccounted for disappearances on Illimani. In reality, he would don a disguise and make his way by road to the border. There he would stop at Cococabana, near Peru. He was to wait at a hotel where his pseudonym had already been booked. When word came, he was to collect the deceased body of Bormann and take it by boat up to Panama City.

Fancy that, he was the one to finally put down the last of Hitler's personal attendants. His father, long since passed on, the man who brought him into the 'trade' as a member of the Maquis, would be smiling in heaven. The only shame was that Bormann would never know. His doctor would see him slipping away, and declare that some unknown disease had brought him low.

As Jean-Paul wiped down the room where he had stayed these past weeks, packed up the equipment, and made ready to store it in the secret location, he considered that it was all for the best.

After all, you can't have everything.

Connecticut 1976

The Final Act

This last story had taken most of the day. Alan Wood-Thomas had at last finished his longest, and only, detailed explanation of what happened 'on the road' so to speak. The night was reaching into the ending of the day, and it was time for rest, but the father's eyes were bright. He seemed to be happy that at last someone knew the full story. Cyrus, listening intently the whole time, had not noticed an entire day had passed. He had felt as if he was there. "Seriously, you got Bormann? And no one ever knew?"

"When the body arrived in Panama, it was checked. The matter took two months. After the funeral, the man's body was preserved, can you imagine it? He wanted to preserve his body like the Egyptians, and then it was placed into a Crypt specially prepared for him. And that was another thing, there was a release lever INSIDE the damn mausoleum, as if Bormann thought he was going to rise from the dead.

"The arrogance of these Nazis was just beyond belief. Regardless, the body was inspected, tested, and known conditions were looked for and found. A break in the collarbone, the teeth, all pretty much proved we got our man. I received the details of all this in a coded message, along with a check, written by some Jewish foundation in New York.

"From what I understood, Bormann was left in lime till the body was just a skeleton, and it was then planted back into Berlin, and buried where it was to be found a year later. It appeared that certain people wanted the remaining Nazis in South America to know what could happen to them. Personally, I see Jacques' hand at work in this.

"Again, it is the art of deception. Convince the enemy that things are here, while they are really there. All those years that we worked together, the Nazi who were hiding in secret never knew when the knife of justice would separate them from their bodies.

"Jacques defeated them in their MINDS, Cyrus, in their minds. He made sure that their paranoia and fear ate into any enjoyment they might have had in their fading years. If we could do this to Bormann, and make it like he never had a life outside of Nazi Germany, then we could do this to any one of them."

Alan was quiet for a moment, so Cyrus asked him, "Did you ever see Jacques again?"

"No, not even in dreams." And with this, Alan Wood-Thomas closed his eyes. He never spoke of the matter of his Nazi hunting again, nor indicated to Cyrus that he wanted to speak further on the subject.

Lou Gehrig's Disease had ruined the body, but the mind was still sharp and clear. But now, his time here was finished. The story has been told, the next generation had heard of what had been done on their behalf.

"Dad, really, do you still hold out that there is nothing past this life? Do you truly believe, after all the incredible things you have done, that that is IT? You are done when you take your last breath?" his son asked.

Alan roused himself, smiling at the boys insistence. He had kissed the damn Bishops ring, he had seen the wealth dripping off the man while the poor were starving. There was no God in any religion that he had ever seen "Tell you what son, if I wake up on the other side, you will have proven me wrong, and I will come back to let you know, OK?"

Little Cy just nodded.

Alan Wood-Thomas, beloved father and husband, respected and recognised artist, and Psychic Nazi Hunter passed away soon after.

Alan Wood-Thomas at Connecticut circa late 1960's

The Kiss

First Day of July, 1976 - 2 AM - Connecticut

The house was quiet, the family sound asleep. They all knew it was not long now. Annabelle wakes, she feels a strange sensation, and knows she must get down to see Alan. As soon as she walks in, she understands: It is his time. She pauses and contemplates the horror of the last year, watching her husband fade. As the condition worsened, his muscles started deteriorating, until now, where he looked like one of the starving Jews they found in the concentration camps.

He looks up, the eyes straining to even focus, so little control has he left over his body, but his hand indicates for her to come close. She does, and with tears in her eyes, she bends down to kiss him. As she does, she feels the return of his abiding affection, deep and true. Just one final kiss, and he is gone.

Lou Gehrig's disease is currently an untreatable condition for allopathic (western) medicine. It was perhaps part of the reason that drove his son, Cyrus, to become a Doctor of Chiropractic and a Homeopath. The nerve cells break down, slowly causing paralysis, or more correctly, atrophy.

Your brain can't send messages to your muscles anymore. Because the muscles don't get any signals, they become very weak. In time, the muscles no longer work and you lose control over their movement.

At first, your muscles get weak or stiff. You may have more trouble with fine movements, such as trying to button a shirt or turn a key. You may stumble or fall more than usual. After a while it just gets worse, and you can't even move your arms, legs, head, or body.

Eventually, people with this disease (Amyotrophic Lateral Sclerosis - ALS) lose control of their diaphragm, the muscles in the chest that help you breathe. Then they can't breathe on their own and will need to be on a breathing machine. Worse, they lose control of the neck muscles, and they can choke on a cramped windpipe if the head falls in the wrong angle. It is not a pleasant thing to witness, especially in a loved one.

Cyrus had connected with a spiritual understanding during these long months as he sat with his father and listened to his stories. He had begun a spiritual practice that would help him leave his body and travel inwardly, not to find Nazis, but instead to find inner truth and understanding. He was sitting up in the room at the time, contemplating, and he felt he could hear the gasping breath of his father. It faltered, then stopped.

With compassion, Cyrus prayed for his soul. Leaving this world after suffering such a horrid disease is a blessing. He felt there was one last message his father wanted to share, and as he felt the great man's spirit, inwardly he saw it happen. His father slipped away. He cried, not tears of pain, but tears for his release. And in his inner vision he felt the love flowing out, but not just from his father, he felt the love from the thousands of voices silenced by the Nazi.

He swears a light entered the room, a soft light, like a door had opened to a beautiful world, and the radiance from that realm spilled out into this one.

He saw it clearly: They were here, those dispossessed, murdered souls, they were HERE. They came to greet his father, their one bright light who led them through the darkness. And finally, he understood, it was not anger that drove his father, it was not violence that brought the visions, it was the compassion. A deep, abiding compassion for those who could not help themselves. He was no avenging angel, nor a judge, Alan Wood-Thomas was just the messenger ... He simply passed on the location of those who murdered these lost Souls, as they who had been murdered had passed it on to him in the only way they could.

In his visions.

The circle was complete.

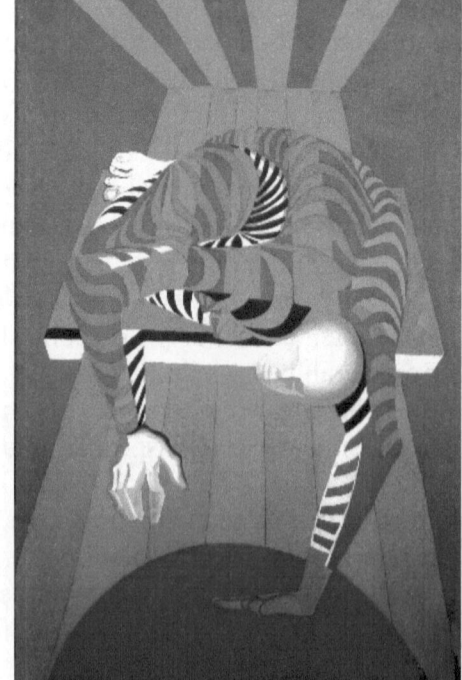

I do not believe in God; his existence has been disproved by Science. But in the concentration camp, I learned to believe in men.

Jean Paul Sartre

Author Note:

How true is this story? This I do not believe is the correct question to ask. What I prefer to think about is the notion: *how much does this tale reveal to us something of our possibilities?* This is more what I am inclined to believe in, that inside each of us lies our individual capacity for greatness. For what it is worth, I have absolutely no doubt that the substance and basic details contained in this book are reasonably accurate. This comes not only from outer confirmed sources, as well as information from Alan's son, Cyrus, but also from 'visions' that came to me when I agreed to write this novel.

However, the turning point of belief for me was when I read *"Secret Soldiers"* by Phillip Gerard. This is when it hit me. Here was external confirmation of so many small details, and as I found the little things start into click into place, it made the larger things much easier to swallow.

As one example: The very fact that Alan Wood-Thomas was able to go into Nazi occupied Paris, and is historically proven to have done so, this told me that perhaps him helping with the arrangements for the surrender of that city was indeed plausible.

The section on Bormann, again, this is in part conjecture, in part based on what was known. Alan did speak to his son of his visions, but in many cases, given the years that have passed, we find that we are piecing together the snippets to make sense of the whole. I used this section of the book as an exercise to largely show *how* the process of revealing someone's true identity was worked out. The scenario, as outlined in this book, is plausible, though obviously not confirmed.

Keep in mind that this project stretched over a twenty-five year period, and that Jacques (actual name unknown) had at least five men on call for the work. Yet for the entire time, none of the agents ever met each other, or any other operative in the field, other than Jacques. Not even his most trusted secretaries had physical contact with an agent.

All that is known is that during the entire time, up to the close of business, not one person was caught or jailed. There was the one time when proper protocols were not followed by a new agent, right towards the end, which could have made the closing of this saga a very different story. This is possibly part of the reason the whole operation shut down. It strikes me that it could have been a combination of many things, not the least being that the visions finally stopped. But the true reality is most likely that the former Maquis operatives who were dedicated to the purpose simply died out. It all ended in 1970, some six years before Allan's death.

People had finally ceased to care about the Nazi and World War Two, and only the Mossad alongside well-funded justice crusaders, such as Wiesenthal, were left in the field.

After extensive discussion with Alan's son, Cyrus, I reconstructed this work, and I will admit, during the process, I was very surprised to be given "visions", as Alan would call them, on very specific and curious points in the story. When I got back to Cyrus, he said these things I was seeing were indeed entirely possible, but that he was not completely certain.

Specifically, the use of Alan Wood-Thomas to broker a deal between Von Choltitz and the Allies in surrendering Paris. The fact Alan was in Paris prior to the surrender is clearly documented in "Secret Soldiers", but the author did not personally interview Alan himself, or his son. However, the stark reality that a non-French battalion was specifically used to liberate Paris.

Added to the relatively easy surrender, and the fact that Von Choltitz refused to follow Hitler's orders to destroy the place, I believed this combination of known facts reveal not just the distinct plausibility, but an absolute certainty of arrangements being made that are not openly known to the historical record. Plus, Von Choltitz himself essentially indicates there was an arrangement in his own book "Is Paris Burning?"

The one thing that "got" me into writing this tale in the first place started some fifteen years prior to it being written. A personal friend, (Cyrus) a man I had known for many years, suddenly wants to talk about his father. I saw the incredible art work the man produced, a true master at work, and then he mentioned the dark under-belly, the Psychic Assassin.

Our connection is that we are both members of a teaching where out-of-the-body projection, lucid dreaming, and 'seeing" the invisible were common place. But to connect this ability to a desire to murder another human being seemed so totally opposed to the entire notion of spirituality and spiritual freedom that I got fascinated. It was a dichotomy. His story got me hooked, but as I say, it would be another fifteen years before I would write it down.

I ask that you view this book as fiction because there is nothing in here that can be objectively proven. However, if you feel there is more truth underlying this, then you would have a foot in my camp. I do believe what Cyrus told me. I do believe his father was telling the truth.

And if nothing else, it makes for the most fabulous tale.

Why Did So Many Nazis Go Unpunished?

Essay By Cyrus Wood-Thomas (Son of Alan Wood-Thomas)

People often ask why so few Nazis were punished for their part in the Holocaust. In July 2008, Jonathan Freedland wrote an article in The Guardian, a U.K. newspaper, entitled "Revenge," in which he cited some interesting statistics. *"After the war, allied officials identified 13.2 million men in western Germany alone as eligible for automatic arrest because they had been deemed part of the Nazi apparatus. Fewer than 3.5 million of these were charged and, of those, 2.5 million were released without trial. That left about a million people - and most of them faced no greater sanction than a fine or confiscation of property that they had looted, a temporary restriction on future employment, or a brief ban from seeking public office.*

"By 1949, four years after the war, only 300 Nazis were in prison. From an original wanted list of 13 million, just 300 paid anything like a serious price."

All told, only 24 individuals were punished at the Nuremberg trials, but it took a whole lot more than 24 people to systematically kill over six million individuals. Literally millions of Nazis and their collaborators went unpunished, people who rounded up the Jews and herded them into railroad cars meant for freight, people who drove the trains and manned the ghettos, work camps and death camps, people who administered the gas, people who shaved heads, people who placed the bodies in incinerators, people who picked out the gold fillings from the ashes - all went unpunished. As well, there were those who profited from the mass killings by selling human hair from Jewish corpses to make felt to line soldiers' boots, reselling precious objets d'art privately owned by Jews, and selling supplies meant for Jewish prisoners on the Black Market.

In Freedland's article, historian David Cesarani, a leading authority on the events of the Holocaust, is quoted as saying that legally punishing all of these people after the war would have been a never-ending task. "Pursuing all those responsible for the slaughter of the Jews would have meant trying thousands upon thousands of people—and it would have ended in the jailing of almost the entire adult male population of Germany."

It wasn't just the Nazis who were to blame for the torture and genocide of the Jews. There were millions of collaborators, some who openly aided the Nazis and others who merely stood by and watched as their neighbors were rounded up and taken away, their property looted and businesses closed or confiscated. The opportunity to do violence to Jews had brought to the surface a hidden anger, a deep, buried hatred that existed within the hearts of many European citizens.

It was a hatred that was so deeply buried that many of them were not even aware of it. The laws against the Jews suddenly gave them permission to act on their darkest fears, perhaps even surprising some of those who thought of themselves as decent, loving people. Starting in 1995, President Jacques Chirac, the National Assembly of France, the French police, the Catholic Church, and certain professional associations acknowledged the extent to which the Vichy government and ordinary French citizens collaborated with the Nazis and actively participated in the Holocaust.

In a number of European countries, there was a great backlash after the war against those who had collaborated with Nazis, and nowhere was this more evident than in France, where historians now acknowledge that at least 10,000 collaborators were summarily executed in the days following the liberation of Paris. Some of these "extrajudicial executions" are now acknowledged to be the work of individuals, while many others were organized by groups of Jews, like the Nokmim, known in English as "Avengers." More can be found about the Avengers in Jonathan Freedland's book, The Final Reckoning.

Many foreign visitors to the United States have commented in various ways on the fact that Americans seem to be among the most law-abiding people on earth. Perhaps this is why so many Americans have trouble coming to terms with the idea that a group of individuals could decide that escaped Nazis and anyone who collaborated with them should be automatically put to death and that if the government wouldn't do it, they would do it.

In my opinion, anyone who asks how it was possible for Alan's group to commit murder under these circumstances is simply not in touch with what actually happened in France after the war. When you consider how few people were punished by the courts, it seems obvious why Alan and his friends decided to kill the men highlighted in Alan's visions, rather than turning them in to the police.

The protocols of the group of assassins may have been thought out all at once, or they may have evolved over time. The general view is that most likely they simply carried on from where they left off in the Maquis. Because their operations continued for so many years and the group was never connected to any of the murders, you could argue that the protocols must have been pretty airtight. I recall my father insisting that no information was written down for long and that only knives were used for the assassinations.

I also recall a time that he asked me to take a message to the library and leave it like a bookmark in a certain reference book. I knew what it was for, and was so frightened that I didn't look at the message, but even if I had, I assume it would have been in code. He must have thought I wouldn't make a very good operative because he never asked me to do anything else of that nature.

People ask me if I truly believe the stories he told me, about the Psychic Nazi Killer who acted in secret for over twenty-five years, tracking down and arranging for the execution of those guilty of war crimes. I don't really answer them, in part because what I believe does not matter, but largely because my opinion does not alter the facts.

But for the record? Yes.

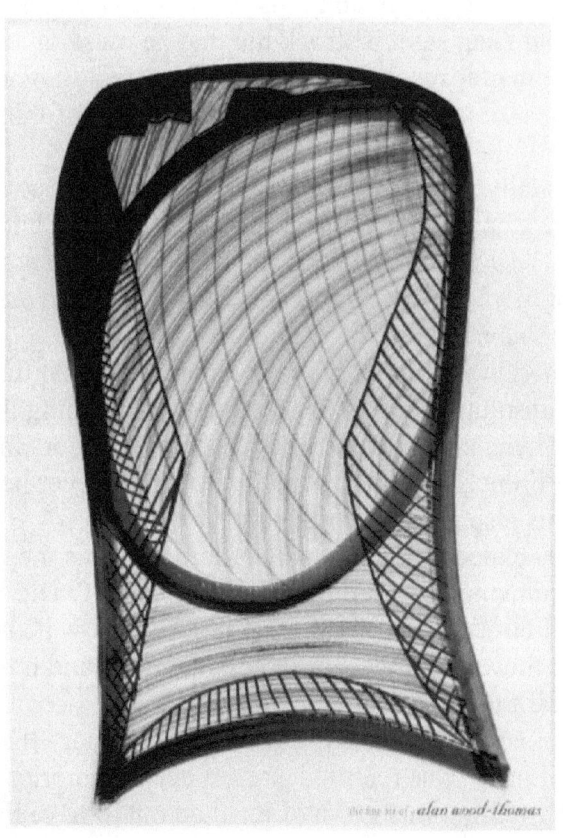

It's the well-behaved children that make the most formidable revolutionaries. They don't say a word, they don't hide under the table, they eat only one piece of chocolate at a time. But later on, they make society pay dearly.

Jean-Paul Sartre

MUNICH

(Note by Cyrus Wood-Thomas)

When I first saw the film 'Munich' by Stephen Spielberg I had tremendous flashbacks to matters I had virtually forgotten. I remembered clearly that as the news of the massacre came onto the news, I was with him, and he said, "If we had been allowed to handle this, only the terrorists would have died."

At the time I just thought this was another odd thing my father was talking about, but when I saw the film, it hit home. He really meant it. Everything he told me, things I felt at the time were mostly fiction, they were real. But it meant more than this. *"If we had been allowed,"* he said, clearly. It struck me that he, or his group, must have been deeply connected to more than just random visions.

Jacques (not his real name, no-one actually knows it) was definitely very well connected to the French Government and must have had German associates as well. From what Alan said, it struck me that he must have put in an application to have the matter resolved, and had it rejected. In other words, this group of assassins was entrenched in the background of things. They were known, and part of the framework.

But the next thing he casually mentioned was the part that really got me thinking. At the time, after we had finished watching the TV report, and perhaps a day later, he said, *"We would not have lost a single innocent life. Our men would have gotten in and been set up, then used snipers on the terrorists, all at the same moment."*

Now whether he had experienced one of his visions on how to do this, I don't know, but he seemed absolutely certain on the matter. The thing that always stuck in my mind: when he spoke to me about serious matters like this, he always dropped the French Accent. I don't think anyone ever heard him speak without it, and this also got me wondering.

Was that part of him that related to me, the part of him that was the Assassin, was this person someone divorced from his natural self? Did he have a *'second self'* inside? I honestly do not know, but I DO know he was crystal clear on the fact that they could have sorted out Munich, and no innocents would have died, if they had been allowed in.

The reality is, I just don't know. But this experience, this memory that came to me after the film 'Munich' was released, stirred deep memories within my Soul. More than anything this is why I reached out to have this story of my remarkable father told.

POST SCRIPT

Many years after his father had passed on, Cyrus was greeted by a woman he knew, the sister of John Clellon Holmes, who was well known to the family. (Her brother used to edit Annabelle's books, and the Wood-Thomas family regularly visited John at Old Saybrook, where his sister often visited at the same time) She said she had a message from Alan, that Alan had repeated several times to her when she saw him on the inner.

Alan had come to her in a Lucid Dream, and asked her to speak to Cyrus, his son, and say - *"Please tell him Alan says: You ALL were right!"* (referring to the families belief in an after-life)

I found that quite extraordinary, firstly because clearly he was not burning in Hell for his crimes, but also that Alan Wood-Thomas was finally prepared to admit he may have been wrong about the after-life.

*To think new thoughts,
you have to break the
bones in your head.*

Jean-Paul Sartre

Doctor Cyrus Wood-Thomas DC

I first met Cyrus on an internet chat group. I liked his humor, his wit, and his sharp ability to see the truth behind what people meant. Plus, he was fun. I had no idea what he did, and it turned out that Cyrus is a *doctor of chiropractic medicine with specialties in classical Homeopathy, blood testing and Nutrition.*

As chance would have it, around this time my voice had completely vanished, and I asked him on line if there were a remedy that might help. He wrote back suggesting a specific remedy. The woman over the road sold Homeopathics, so I went and got what he prescribed. The voice returned within the hour.

I was impressed, but even more so when I looked up that specific remedy, and found there was nothing in the books at all that indicated for it to be used in this circumstance. I asked him why he selected it, and Cyrus said, "Did it work?" I said it did, so he added, "So why do you want to question it?"

It was some years later that he mentioned to me that he had had a sort of epiphany. After watching the film 'Munich', he had vivid recall of his father. and felt the Alan Wood-Thomas story needed to be told. He described it, loosely, and I said, "Well, if you want it written up, let me know." It took perhaps fifteen years for him to get back to me on the subject. When we finally got underway Cyrus was an extraordinary help in clarifying things, the small details and the time lines, etc. He also assisted in going over possible story lines as they evolved, and generally affirming that things were moving in the right direction.

He is available to comment or further questions about his father and you are welcome to write if you wish to know more.

He is available for comment or further questions about his father and you are welcome to write if you wish to know more: info@woodthomas.com

Cyrus would love this project to turn into a TV series or film and would be especially excited to talk about the possibility.

Alan Wood-Thomas relaxing in his studio circa late 1950's

Author Addendum

The substance of this book was written in just three months. Normally such a project, with all the necessary research, would take three years, but again and again, pages on books would fall open at the right spot. I would walk into a library, and find a rare book sitting on a shelf, which gave specific answers to questions I was asking.

Plus, all through the process I was given "visions". Pristine and clear insights into such things as the Assassin's suitcase, how funding for the project was achieved, and so many minute details regarding many of the events surrounding the book. I came to the conclusion that Alan Wood-Thomas WANTED his story told. There were far too many coincidences for it to be accidental.

In all, I began to feel a part of the Wood-Thomas family, even though I had not personally met any of them. As I finished up the book, I was invited to a 'party' on the Inner Planes, such as Cyrus described the family always had every weekend. There they all were, handing out the food, laughing, smiling. I felt a tremendous zest for life running through everyone present. I took it as an affirmation that the general principles in the book were sound, and that there was an approval of the work.

I would like to thank Cyrus Wood-Thomas for his contributions and ongoing assistance in clarifying points as they came up. Also the earlier work on this subject, "Remote Assassin" written by Linda LeBoutiller, served as a focus.

Thank you for travelling with me on this journey, a book such as this is a rare event, and a privilege to write.

Alan Wood-Thomas attending an art show in New York City, circa early 1960's

Victims of Spoliations

It is possible to get reparation for assets spoliated in France during the war (shop, apartments, etc...). This program concerns the victims themselves or their heirs. This reparation extends to certain Jews spoliated in Tunisia.

Movable and Financial Spoliation

The CIVS, commission pour l'indemnisation des victimes de spoliation (commission for the compensation of victims of spoliation) was set up under the recommendation of the Mattéoli Commision, by the decree #99-778 of September 10, 1999, modified by the decree #2000-932 of September 25, 2000 and is in charge of reviewing the individual applications presented by the victims or their heirs for the reparation of damages caused by spoliation of assets because of the anti-Semitic legislation enforced during the Occupation by the occupier and the Vichy authorities.

The Commission is not a jurisdiction and is in charge of developing appropriate measures for reparation or compensation. It can express any useful recommendation, especially in terms of compensation.

These recommendations are then sent to the General Secretary of the Government. Under the decree of September 10, 1999, only damages caused by spoliation of material and financial assets give right to reparations, restitution or compensation. Moral damages are not covered by this reparation program.

For example, spoliation may concern furniture or valuables in an apartment that was looted, but also professional equipment related to a craft activity or to a business. Additionally, only spoliation that happened because of the anti-Semitic legislation enforced during the Occupation by the occupier and by Vichy authorities are concerned.

In 10 years, CIVS reviewed 24,000 applications and allocated nearly 450 million Euros of reparations.

>Applications should be sent to:
>C.I.V.S.
>1 Rue de la Manutention
>75116 PARIS
>Website : www.civs.gouv.fr (available in 4 languages)

About the Artist:

Alan Wood-Thomas was born in Paris in the 1920's. He started his career in Art at a very young age and continued his pursuit of every more perfect works all the way up until his death in 1976.

Over the years he had become a very prominent and respected painter with many of his masterpieces having been showcased in some renowned gallery's: *The Whitney Museum of American art in New York, The Art Institute of Chicago, the Tokyo Museum of Modern Art (which is now the National Museum of modern Art), the Tel Aviv Museum of art in Tel Aviv, Israel and the Fransworth Museum in Rockland, Maine.*

In 1968 Alan was commissioned by the justice department to do the portrait of *Nicholas deB. Katzenbach*, former Under Secretary of State to Kennedy and former Attorney General. The portrait hangs on the fifth floor of the Justice Department to this very day.

At the time of his death in 1976 Alan had left over 700 masterpieces - 1500 pen and ink drawings - and 300 etchings to his family - twelve of these etchings were a series entitled 'The Deaths of Picasso' - which are by far some of the most beautiful pieces he had ever created.

You can view some of these images as a testimony to this mans unique vision of the reality we live - so that it may be remembered - and in turn stand the test of time. If you would like more information on the artist or would like to view some more of this fine art a website has been created to do just that - www.woodthomas.com.

Other Books by this Author

Hello Planet Earth

This is an utterly delightful tale of a child discovering his truth. Set as a series of short vignettes, this book is simply a joy to read.

Available on Amazon or through laddertothemoon.com.au

The Boringbar War

A remarkable saga of a Supreme Court, Divorce, Incest, Lies and Deceit that was written in just THREE DAYS by the Author. Based on actual events, names have been changed to protect the guilty.

Available on Amazon or through laddertothemoon.com.au

RATOLOGY: Books I and II

Writing into a newsgroup embroiled in constant and heated argument way back at the dawn of the web, Michael diffused the anger with wisdom from the Great Rat. People kept telling the author he should record his truth-filled yet ironic statements of the obvious as a book. He went one step further, and turned them into the worlds FIRST GENUINELY ARTIFICIAL RELIGION.

Available on Amazon or through laddertothemoon.com.au

The Book of Number Series

Available on Amazon

Have you ever felt that there was something more?

The ancient art of Divination by Number is an extraordinary study you may wish to contemplate. The author of this book has written a complete course on "how to do" Pythagorean Numerology. In just WEEKS you can discover and understand so much about the numerical secrets of the Ancient Greeks, much of it not available in other books.

The "Book of Number" is a series of three books that cover the whole teaching of Number Divination as taught by the Ancient Pythagoreans. They are available on Amazon or direct from the author. Details are on the web-page (below) if you wish to know more.

Laddertothemoon.com.au

For further enquiries and updates go to the official web page at laddertothemoon.com.au.

You may also write to info.numberharmonics@gmail.com.

There are variations to the Numerology books with the Dice Divination series, (same author) as well as workshops books, and other teaching aids for those interested in furthering their knowledge in this area.

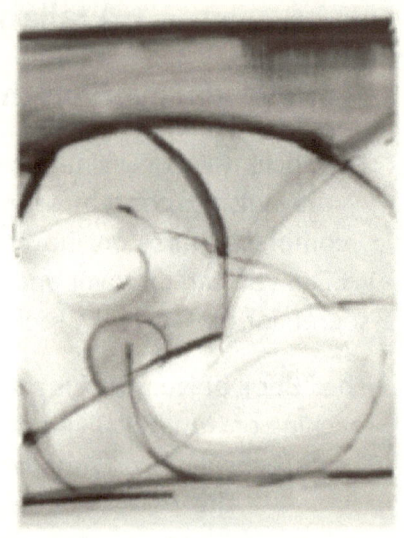

Psychic Nazi Hunter

COPYRIGHT 2017 Michael Wallace

This book is published under the Berne Convention. All rights are reserved. Apart from any fair dealing for the purpose of private study, research, criticism or review, as permitted under the Copyright Act, 1966, no part of this publication may be reproduced, stored in a retrieval system, or transmitted, in any form or by any means, electronic, electrical, chemical, mechanical, optical, photocopying, recording or otherwise, without the prior permission of the copyright holder. Enquiries should be send to the publishers at the under-mentioned email address.

ISBN: 978-0-9941798-5-2
Copyright 2017 Michael Wallace
Publisher: Ladder to the Moon Productions
Email: info.numberharmonics@gmail.com
Web: laddertothemoon.com.au

www.ingramcontent.com/pod-product-compliance
Lightning Source LLC
Chambersburg PA
CBHW030905170426
43193CB00009BA/742